Come, Journey With Me:
A Personal Story of
Conversion and Ordination

Come, Journey With Me: A Personal Story of Conversion and Ordination

Russell C. Packard

AFFIRMATION BOOKS
WHITINSVILLE, MASSACHUSETTS

Nihil obstat
Very Rev. Todd O. Hevia, J.C.D.
Censor Deputatus

Imprimatur
Rene H. Gracida
Bishop of Corpus Christi
Former Bishop of Pensacola-Tallahassee
30 March 1982

First Edition

© 1984 by Russell C. Packard

All rights reserved, including the right of reproduction in whole or in part, in any form or by any means, electronic or mechanical, including photocopying, or by any information storage and retrieval system, without permission in writing from the publisher. Inquiries should be addressed to Editor, Affirmation Books, 22 The Fenway, Boston, MA 02215.

Scripture texts used in this work are taken from the New American Bible, copyright © 1970, by the Confraternity of Christian Doctrine, Washington, D.C., and are used by permission of the copyright owner. All rights reserved.

Library of Congress Cataloging in Publication Data
Packard, Russell C.
  Come, Journey With Me.
  1. Packard, Russell C. 2. Converts, Catholic—United States—Biography. 3. Deacons—Catholic Church—Biography. I. Title.
BX4668.P23A34 1984   248.2'46'0924 [B]   84-24356
ISBN 0-89571-021-8

Printed by
Mercantile Printing Company, Worcester, Massachusetts
United States of America

Contents

Foreword 7

Preface 9

Dedication 11

Introduction: in the beginning... 13

Chapter 1   Early stirrings 17

Chapter 2   First steps 27

Chapter 3   Conflict 34

Chapter 4   Falling in love 40

Chapter 5   Bread and wine 48

Chapter 6   A calling 55

Chapter 7   A new Christian 64

Chapter 8   Learning 70

Chapter 9   Prayer 88

Chapter 10 In the desert 98

Chapter 11 Struggles, failures, goodbyes 112

Chapter 12 Sin and spiritual direction 123

Chapter 13 A physician prays for healing 132

Chapter 14	Doctor and deacon	141
Chapter 15	Questions	153
Chapter 16	A new beginning: on retreat	163
Chapter 17	Who am I?	170
Chapter 18	Come aside for a while	177
Chapter 19	Reflections on the journey	182
Chapter 20	Tomorrow is forever	194

Foreword

Come, Journey With Me by Russell Packard, M.D., is a story in journal form of a navy psychiatrist and neurologist's conversion to Catholicism and ordination to the diaconate. A long-professed atheist, believing only in the powers of science, the author is shocked to discover his own spiritual stirrings after the death of a patient. As a psychiatrist he tries to explain them away, and yet something in him convinces him to trust his new feelings.

With the affirmation of his wife and a priest friend, the author struggles with his new identity of "believer," an identity which often feels at odds with that of "professional." At times he is doubtful about the thought of baptism, at other times he wants to jump right in, so overtaken is he by his own enthusiasm. Very shortly after his baptism, despite urgings of caution not to act too soon, he begins a two-year course of study to become a deacon in the Church.

This decision by no means ends his struggling and questioning, and yet, despite his doubts, the program brings him much joy. It is this joy and struggle that we share as we reflect on the words of this book by Dr. Packard. And it is particularly appropriate that Affirmation Books publish *Come, Journey With Me* during this moment in history when the role of the permanent deacon is becoming more understood and appreciated.

The deacon brings to his ministry, no matter what its particular application, an added dimension which the layperson does not bring to the service of others; the deacon has the charism and grace of the sacrament of Orders. The deacon in our midst is a constant reminder of the spiritual and sacramental character of the Church's work and mission. The struggle and growth of this one deacon as portrayed in this book wil help us to better appreciate the divine and beautiful gifts of the Holy Spirit bestowed on the people of God.

> Thomas A. Kane, Ph.D., D.P.S.
> Priest, Diocese of Worcester
> Publisher, Affirmation Books
> Boston, Massachusetts

19 October 1984
Feast of St. Luke the Physician

Preface

From the time of the conversion of Saint Paul and *The Confessions of St. Augustine* to the present, men and women have found a certain fascination in reading of another's spiritual journey from unbelief to belief. No matter how different the experience there will always be those incidents, those moments in the other's journey wherein we can see ourselves, recall our own experience, and contrast their and our reactions to similar circumstances. Even when there is little or no similarity in our experience of conversion there is always the challenge of trying to imagine how we would have acted or reacted under similar circumstances.

Dr. Russell Packard's account of his journey from unbelief to ordination to the diaconate is one that will hold the interest of the reader, not only because of the candor with which he has described his journey, but also because he describes the journey of a scientist. In our day, when the full impact of the progress made in the latter half of the twentieth century by science and technology is being felt in a negative way in the area of the moral life of humans, the conversion of a man of science to a man of faith who is still dedicated to the practice of medicine is indeed an encouraging sign.

There is something here, then, for everyone: the believer, the doubter; the saint, the sinner!

> Rene H. Gracida
> Bishop of Corpus Christi
> Former Bishop of Pensacola-Tallahassee

Dedication

Life is God's gift to us. What we do with it is our gift to God. I would like to share this gift of writing with, and dedicate it to, several friends and companions who accompanied and often guided me on this journey.

First of all I must thank Gretchen, who has been my constant loving companion. She, above all, was always there when I lost sight of my way and felt alone. Also, I thank Father Patrick Fryer, who introduced me to the beautiful mystery of the bread and wine; the late Father Leo Burns, who guided me into a life of prayer; Father Fausto Stampiglia, director of the permanent diaconate training program, who said, "Come, stay with us;" and Bishop Rene Gracida, who I believe had more faith in me than I had in myself.

I also thank Jana, Becky, and Laura who shared the typing tasks of putting this journey on paper, along with Dr. and Mrs. Robert Saxer, Father Bob Mazur, Father Robert Rimes, S.J., and Reverend Denny Taylor for their help and advice in reviewing portions of the manuscript.

Russell C. Packard
Pensacola, Florida

Introduction
In the beginning...

God chose those whom the world considers absurd to shame the wise; he singled out the weak of this world to shame the strong. He chose the world's lowborn and despised, those who count for nothing, to reduce to nothing those who were something; so that mankind can do no boasting before God.   (Corinthians 1:27-29)

In the beginning I did not believe. I can easily say I never really thought about God in any meaningful way until I was thirty-one. I am now thirty-five.

As a child I went to Sunday School twice. The first time occurred when the local pastor came to my parents' door and asked them please to send me. I didn't want to go but my mother finally sent me off one cold Sunday morning, wearing a little red knitted hat. I listened to the Bible stories in a rather distant way and on the way home one of the boys from the class took my hat and threw it over a fence. I cried all the way home and refused to go back. About a year later I returned at the urging of a friend because his church was having a Halloween party. I wore a devil costume and got a nosebleed when I had a fight with an angel.

Through high school and college I though it was fashionable to argue against the existence of God. It was a simple argument—no one could prove anything. As a medical student I became an intellectual snob: who needed religion? I felt I had the answer for everything—at least everything medical.

In 1970 I entered the navy to avoid the "doctor draft." I never guessed I would spend the next ten years there, seven of which were dedicated to advanced residency training in psychiatry and neurology. When I became a psychiatrist my thinking evolved to a higher level: religion was neurosis, a crutch for those who could not stand on their own two feet. I even recall keeping chaplains away from my patients because I didn't see how they could possibly help.

During my neurology training I realized that religious visions were simply electrical discharges in the brain and could be treated with the proper medication. I did become more charitable at that point, accepting the idea that religion was all right for those who needed it. I certainly didn't need it.

My first marriage ended in divorce; I guess I didn't have the answer to that one. For nearly a year I floundered, isolating myself, chasing women, and living in a small Bachelor Officers Quarters room with only my books, some clothes, and a spoon. If I had known about the Exodus experience, I would have realized that I was in the desert lying on my face, but unlike Moses, I never looked up. The thought of spiritual salvation never occured to me.

Seasons change and life began to improve again with the warmth of spring. I was chief resident in neurology and in a few short months I would be a staff neurologist at a new naval hospital. I met an attractive woman, Gretchen, who was Catholic. We fell in love and decided to marry. I respected her faith and agreed to obtain an annulment of my previous marriage and marry her in the Church. But I adamantly refused to become a Catholic simply because she was one. Quite wisely, she never pushed the issue.

Such was the state of my life when one lonely night I was struggling with a dying patient. In sheer frustration with my own limitations I reached out for something, anything to help me. I was answered by a faint stirring in the depths of my spirit, a stirring that was to become for me the first step on an inward journey into faith. Simultaneously, I was moved to begin writing, without understanding at first, but as if I had an inner awareness that a door was slowly opening into a new life, one that included writing.

Over the next three years I captured on paper the process of my own conversion and a call to ministry as a permanent deacon in the Roman Catholic Church. But most of all, a personal and very intimate story of a developing relationship began to unfold, almost a stormy love affair with God. Like most relationships it was not particularly love at first sight, but an arousing of curiosity and interest, followed by a series of highs and lows. I did not fall in love passively and without difficulty. I struggled. I often tried to "break it off," but I couldn't. I went on, uncertain, but growing and following, learning to love.

During this unexpected journey I became almost painfully aware that behind my white coat and stethoscope was a very ordinary man, often weak, foolish, stubborn, and filled with questions, doubts, and fears. As I continued to write I began to question what such an ordinary man could offer by sharing this inner journey with others. I was neither wise nor famous. I was not a known writer nor a theologian. I was certainly not a saint—I didn't even know how to pray. I slowly began to realize that I was writing for the very reason that I am ordinary. Most of us, although we strive for perfection or even pretend to be profound and important, are all basically pretty ordinary, and a spiritual life often seems strangely unobtainable. While Jesus walked on water, we are confined to this earth. We easily forget that he came for the ordinary, the lowly, and the weak. Was there ever a more ordinary group of men than the Apostles?

This book is written, therefore, for others who are also ordinary, who struggle with their own spiritual lives, who, in their hearts, are seeking.

Because the people in this book are all real, I have spared no effort in altering names and physical descriptions to protect their privacy. I admit there are a few who are thinly disguised and some who are not disguised at all, because these people have such a marvelous way of changing lives that their presence should be allowed to shine through.

Chapter 1

Early stirrings

...I have left an open door before you which no one can close.   (Revelation 3:8)

Tuesday evening, January 10, 1978
Pensacola, Florida

    Mrs. Jordan is dead. It seems a strange time to begin writing a book, only moments after one of my patients has died, but for me this has certainly not been an ordinary death. I have seen many patients die. There wasn't anything particularly "special" about this patient. I barely knew her. I am not even sure why I am writing this now but I feel I must. It is very clearly the beginning of something. As her life was slipping away, I felt as though mine were somehow just beginning.
    Mrs. Jordan was wheeled into my office three short days ago. Her husband carefully maneuvered her wheelchair and I knew the moment I saw her shaved head what she had been through. She had a massive, inoperable brain tumor discovered about seven months ago and was treated with radiation therapy and steroids, which helped decrease the brain swelling somewhat but left her extremely

depressed. Her face was pale and puffy from the steroids and her eyes were deep, dark, and uncaring. She wore a scarf over her bare head and was confined to the wheelchair because of a partial paralysis. Her husband was a solid and sincere man, but nearly broken by the agony of his wife's terrible illness. I felt sorry for them both and frustrated with my own sense of helplessness. There was nothing I could do except to start her on a low dose of an antidepressant. Her husband asked if he could call me when she began to get worse and I said, "Of course." He asked me how much time she had and I told him I had no idea. I thought it would probably be a few weeks to a month.

I was surprised when I was called this morning to the emergency room. Mrs. Jordan had taken a turn for the worse. She was almost unresponsive and I had to admit her. I suggested it might be possible that she had deteriorated so suddenly from an infection like pneumonia or a urinary tract infection. Inwardly, I thought her tumor was just breaking out of control.

A few hours later I was surprised to find a whispy infiltrate in the right lung on her chest x-ray. She most likely had early pneumonia. In her condition I didn't know whether to start treatment or not. I remembered the quiet words from medical school echoing through my mind: "Pneumonia is the old man's friend." I decided to have the family-practice resident try to induce a sputum culture and to start antibiotic treatment. I had seen a few brain tumor patients get worse with an infection and return to a few months of useful living after their infection was controlled. We had to try.

Mrs. Jordan's respirations became shallow and she started spiking a fever. We put her on Tylenol suppositories and placed her on a cooling blanket for the fever. I was called an hour later because her temperature was 105 degrees. I went up to the ward immediately and examined her, finding nearly pinpoint pupils and eyes that were staring down at her nose. I felt that she probably had a deep brain hemorrhage or increased pressure from her glioma. I increased her steroids to try to bring down the intracranial pressure.

I went home feeling very alone, frustrated. I tried to call Gretchen in Bethesda but couldn't reach her. I went to bed and fell into a fitful sleep but was jarred awake by the telephone an hour later. Mrs. Jordan had started seizing and the residents didn't know what to do. I didn't either. I kept thinking of how she had looked just three days before, staring at me with those large, sad eyes. I told the residents to treat her with intravenous Valium and call me back. I thrashed around in bed, wondering whether I should start a major anticonvulsant.

I felt extremely frustrated. Six years of post-graduate medical training and I was helpless. I didn't know what to do. For perhaps the first time in my life I reached out. I said, "My God, help me.... I don't know what to do." I didn't get an answer in words, but my anxiety began to melt away. I felt that I could let go, that I didn't have to do anything more. She would be taken care of and I could rest. It was as if God had said, "She is in my hands now. Do not worry." I called the resident back and told him to repeat the Valium injections if she continued to have seizures and said I would come in.

When I arrived, the seizures had stopped and her fever was not so high. I told her husband that we were trying to control the seizures but that things looked ominous. An hour later she peacefully expired. After pronouncing her dead, I stood in the awful silence of that room and looked at her lifeless form. I had never before considered a spiritual side of life but found myself wondering where she was in that silence, whether she was now experiencing the sense of peace of which I had just had the briefest glimpse.

It is as if I have been touched with an awareness I have never felt before, a faint intimation that there may actually be a God.

Wednesday, January 25, 1978

Now that some time has passed since Mrs. Jordan's death, I am not sure what I actually experienced the other night. I am somewhat skeptical, both about what I felt and why I began writing. At the same time, however, I cannot seem to let go of that brief but deep feeling of peace and what seemed to be a sense of caring.

I have to meet with a Father Fryer tomorrow to go over my annulment papers. He sounds like an odd one. When I echoed his name on the phone, he sounded annoyed, "Yes, Fryer, like chicken fryer."

Thursday, January 26, 1978

Something must be happening to me. I met with Father Fryer almost all evening.

We had an awkward start because both of us were a bit defensive and businesslike. As I entered his office, I was confronted with a muscular, somewhat aggressive young priest who was talking on the telephone about a baptism. "Well, if you don't practise your faith, why do you want to have your baby baptized?" As he listened into the receiver he waved at me to sit down and stared at me with his light green eyes. I felt as if he were asking me the same question.

I looked around his office. There was a sign on the wall above his desk saying, *Everyone brings joy to this office, some by entering, some by leaving.* The other walls were covered with posters of popes, golden crosses, and a large modern painting of what looked to be a rather morbid last supper. The priest's desk was cluttered with papers and a pair of jogging shoes. I noticed then that he wasn't wearing shoes. He began writing a note in a colorful orange scrawl and added it to the stack. A note on the corner of the desk next to me read, "Remember, where your treasure is, there your heart is also."

Since most of the actual paperwork was already done, I think he just wanted to get the annulment over with quickly, which was fine with me. I made it clear that I was only marrying Gretchen in the Church because of her belief. As we went through the required and inevitable questions and answers, Father Patrick Fryer's square jaw continued to be set and his green eyes remained solemn and serious. For some reason I became curious about this man with the gold cross on his khaki collar. I suddenly asked him, "What is this God thing that you dedicate your life to all about?" He appeared a bit startled at the question and his mouth began to open. Then he closed it again and began rubbing a small scar at the corner of his mouth. For a second I was sorry I had asked the question. I began to prepare myself to fend off a sermon or an attempt on his part to convert me. I was ready with all my past arguments.

He leaned back in his wooden chair and a small smile played across his face. He slowly shook his head and said, "I almost gave you an answer out of the Baltimore Catechism, but then I knew that wouldn't mean anything to you and at the same time I wasn't sure it would mean anything to me either. My answer, if you really want to know the truth, is that I don't know. God is a mystery."

I didn't have an answer for that one, much less an argument. In fact, I felt slightly intrigued. Never in my life had anyone ever given me an answer like that about God. It was the first time I was faced with someone who didn't try either to shove Jesus down my throat or "save" me. Instead, he actually apologized about his answer and asked me if I would join him for dinner so we could talk some more. Since I was marrying a Catholic woman, he thought if I learned a little about the Church it might enhance our relationship. I agreed, but I was still a bit sorry I had asked the question.

We talked late into the night and I began to feel a subdued excitement—the sensation of a door slowly beginning to open. I shared my recent experience about Mrs. Jordan and found I could identify with this man who didn't have all the answers either. As we parted I felt I was drawing close to him and wanted to return and talk to him again. What was more impressive to me than his words, however, was his belief. He loves his life as a priest, obviously believes in what he speaks about, and attempts to live what he teaches. Curiously, the core of his message, which he said was also that of Jesus, is that faith is a mystery and that Jesus is the center of the mystery. He gave me a book about Jesus that I could read if I wanted to: no pressure.

In some ways I would like to learn more about this Jesus.

Saturday evening, February 25, 1978
Bethesda, Maryland

Gretchen and I were married today at the Bethesda Naval Hospital Chapel. We met at this hospital and have spent most of our waking lives here the past three years, so it seemed only fitting that we should be married here. It was my first time at a Catholic mass and never have I been more aware of being non-Catholic.

Gretchen was beautiful in her flowing white gown. She carried one long-stemmed red rose and was accompanied by her sisters, who wore brightly-colored dresses and smiles on their faces. My closest heathen friends accompanied me. My best man was a very kind but fallen-away Catholic lawyer, who at least knew when to kneel. My ushers consisted of a pleasant, bearded Jewish pediatrician and a not-so-pleasant, bearded neurosurgeon who didn't believe in God and at first refused to stand at the altar. We finally coaxed him to stand with us but he continued to look sour and grind his teeth.

No one from my family came, either because of distance, travel expense, or the bitter cold of the Maryland winter. In my heart I knew there was another, more insidious reason: I was marrying a Catholic woman. Even though many in my family profess some degree of faith, Catholics have never been looked upon kindly. The major question about my marriage had been a rather horrified, "You aren't becoming a Catholic, are you?"

On the other hand, Gretchen's family initially tried very hard to get her to "see the light" about the "previously married sinner" whom she had chosen for her husband. I had been called many things in the process of our courting, some true, some untrue. At one point I was driven to ask Gretchen about the type of God Catholics believed in. I had thought (in my rather simple, unchurched way) that God is supposed to be forgiving and loving. Why did her family hate me so, without even knowing me? She answered simply, "God is as you say he is. My family is merely afraid I will be hurt. But what is most important is what you and I believe." By the time of the marriage her entire family came out of the mountains of Pennsylvania and seemed to accept me with open hearts—even her father, who at one point had roared like a bear at Gretchen about my being her choice. Her mother had to be brought across the street from the hospital at the National Institute of Health where she had been receiving treatment for lung cancer. She looked pale and tired but her tears were tears of joy. Perhaps this is a lesson in faith I have never realized. My family chose the way of ignorance and even bitterness, while Gretchen's family reacted with what I can only describe as faith.

As the ceremony began I felt self-conscious about kneeling; I wasn't used to kneeling but I also had a rather prominent hole in the sole of my shoe. I stared at the large gold cross behind the altar and then fixed my eyes on our wedding candle, a gift from Father Fryer. A young, robed Franciscan priest appeared out of nowhere before the wedding and said he was there to represent Father Fryer and concelebrate the wedding mass. Gretchen and I were both deeply moved by his presence.

"On the cross of the wedding candle are two circles, without beginning, without end...symbolic of God's endless love." As the priest's words passed through my being I was so excited and nervous I could not always follow them, but I felt a stirring of my heart about the mystery of our being brought together in love like this. If there is indeed a God, he must truly be present in our relationship. I also feel that he must have been present at our marriage. Although I remain skeptical, I sense that there is a presence acting in my life now, something I feel almost irresistibly drawn to—like a moth to a flickering flame.

Friday afternoon, March 10, 1978

The honeymoon is over. Gretchen is back in Bethesda and I am back here in Pensacola seeing patients and missing my wife. She does not have orders to come to Pensacola for two more weeks. It's frustrating to be separated but I guess we should be happy that she wasn't given orders to San Diego!

Pat Fryer called me last night and invited me to attend a brief four-week series of bible classes that he is starting this Sunday evening. I said I wasn't sure I could make it but something is tugging at me to learn more. So far my only encounter with the Bible has been to remove it from the room-service menu in hotels.

Friday evening, March 24, 1978

I have now attended two of Pat's bible classes and must admit that I have enjoyed them.

During the first class I planted myself at the back of the small chapel, away from the others, with my arms crossed in a defensive posture. I also refused to pick up one of the Bibles. I just wanted to listen. I couldn't believe I was actually sitting there. My old feelings of God's being some sort of mass neurosis were still with me, but at the same time I was moved by Pat's lesson, which was very inspiring.

It was curious to me that I felt more open to what he was saying than the "cradle" Catholics. They have such a peculiar idea of what scripture means. Even I can see that taking scripture literally is like remaining blind by choice. They could not seem to comprehend the idea that God's love is unconditional. We are the ones who make it conditional; we feel that we have to "do something" for God's love: count beads, repeat prayers, go to church, or do any number of things in order to win God's love. What is the purpose of loving God if we must do all this for his attention? He loves us for what we are but we must let God be God.

At the second class, I unfolded my arms and picked up a Bible, but did not open it. Pat began telling us that growth sometimes causes pain and he was aware that some of the people in the class were having their faith shaken a bit. At one point he said, "Why is it that a dog doesn't have any trouble being a dog, but we have such a terrible time being human?"

He began with the Old Testament, explaining how this group of books deals with God revealing himself to human beings. He said the Bible covers approximately a two-thousand-year period and was written in faith, so it can only be understood in faith. He emphasized that our faith must not be in words, but in God and his son, Jesus. In order to understand scripture, we must understand the people who wrote it. Scripture involves the experience of humans listening to God in their own self-awareness. The words of scripture are Inspired.

At one point, Pat began pacing in front of the room and asked us how often we have listened to God or been aware of his presence for even five minutes. There was a rather peculiar silence.

I decided to take the Bible home. True to form I have not looked at it since. It will probably be the closest I ever come to scripture. At this point I don't have time to read the Bible anyway because I am studying for my neurology board exam, and it takes up every spare moment.

Saturday afternoon, April 8, 1978

My God, I can't believe what's happening. My whole being is changing.

Three days ago something absolutely amazing occurred. For the past two weeks I have practically abandoned all thought about God and religion. On Wednesday I awoke to a bright but cool morning, shaved, and began my morning shower, not thinking about anything. All of a sudden, my mind was filled with the name Ishmael. My immediate response was one of puzzlement. "Ishmael?" I repeated it to myself several times. I wasn't aware that I had ever heard of Ishmael but I knew I would be able to find the word in the Bible.

What surprised me almost more than the name itself was the way it appeared in my stream of consciousness. I suppose an analytic type would say it had been lingering in my unconscious and suddenly burst forth, but I know that timing in psychiatric "revelation" is also extremely important. I asked myself, "Why now?"

I recalled immediately Pat's wordsa, "When God touches us, it is a gift." Even then I did not go to the Bible for three days. But the word never left my mind. It haunted me. I woke up thinking, "Ishmael," and thought of it while I studied neuroanatomy and neuropathology. I continued stubbornly to resist the urge to find it in the Bible until this morning.

I still had the Bible from the class. I picked it up, carried it to my desk, and quietly opened it for the first time. Because Pat had talked about the Bible, I felt that I had some understanding of it as I began to turn the pages. It took me a while to find Ishmael. He was one of Abraham's sons, a "wild ass of a man." (God must know me well.) When I found the literal meaning of Ishmael described in a footnote, I was deeply touched: "God has heard." He had heard me the night I reached out about my patient. I read the words again and tears began to fill my eyes. I thanked God for speaking to me. My God, you are a real God.

Sunday, April 9, 1978

I am on my way to New Orleans now to take the first part of my neurology board exam tomorrow morning. My feelings about yesterday are mixed. All the confidence I had seems to be eroding into self-doubt. In one way I feel that I must have heard the word somewhere before and the whole experience is simply a trick of my imagination, but in the core of my being I feel as if a fire has been kindled that will never go out. Despite my nagging doubts, my heart continues to believe that God has spoken.

Wednesday, April 19, 1978

Things are happening to me that I just don't understand. Gretchen and I are on our way to San Diego now to visit my grandparents. A few minutes ago our flight became a bit turbulent. I was reading the book about Jesus that Pat gave me several months ago. The turbulence grew and the words started jumping around the pages of the book so I laid it down. I found myself trying to pray, or meditate, or just talk with God. For a few seconds I concentrated on smoothing out the flight. The turbulence grew and the pilot turned on the fasten-seat-belt sign, announcing that we were in for several minutes of turbulence. I closed my eyes and asked for God's help. "We can smooth this out; we can do it." Suddenly, the turbulence stopped. We could have been skating on ice. At the same time, I had the peculiar sensation that I had to continue to concentrate and I was beginning to tire. Part of me was elated and I almost called out, "We are doing it!" The seat belt sign winked off. I felt a strange sense of awe and a growing skepticism. This had to be a random event. Why should I be excited about nothing?

I told Gretchen about what had happened and she shook her head. Whatever is happening I feel it is urgent now to continue this writing. Even random events have a way of adding up. I must write and I must write everything in truth, or it will be nothing. Silences, trials and failures, all of my feelings on this journey must be included.

Chapter 2

First steps

...Reform your lives! The reign of God is at hand.
(Matthew 3:2)

Friday evening, April 28, 1978

My conscience has been nagging at me all week. I have been here in California at the navy's expense to attend a neurology meeting and I haven't spent one day at the meeting. Instead, I have flitted around with Gretchen visiting friends and relatives and seeing my children, who live here with my ex-wife.

I don't know what is the matter with me. I have taken business trips before without paying much attention to the work at hand and I have never felt guilty about it.

Sunday, April 30, 1978

I think God has just given me a swift kick in the seat of my pants. An hour ago I was struggling with my conscience about the money I took for the meeting I didn't attend. Our flight home was perfectly smooth this time and Gretchen was napping quietly beside me. Inwardly, I considered the thought of returning the money. I couldn't bring myself to do it: it would be too embarrassing; I couldn't afford it, and so on. My damn conscience continued to nibble away at me until I became irritated and said under my breath, "The hell with it—I'm going to keep it." As I uttered the last word, the plane bounced with a frightening *Wumpf!* It was such a jolt that Gretchen was jarred awake. She looked at me wide-eyed, afraid something was wrong with the plane. I tried to make a joke, saying the pilot had probably just experienced an attack of gas. It didn't work.

I am startled again at the timing of what just happened. I see very clearly that I have been personally shaken. Inwardly, I feel as if I were gently grasped about the shoulders and given a shake. I immediately covered my eyes and prayed silently. I did not feel threatened or that I had been "bad." It was as if someone were saying to me, "Listen to yourself speak—you know where your heart is."

Gretchen and I began to talk because neither of us had ever experienced such a strange pocket of turbulence before. She said it had seemed "almost unnatural." I couldn't tell her how I thought it had come about: she might laugh. Then a few minutes later I had to tell her. She didn't laugh. There were tears in her eyes. I love her.

Monday evening, May 1, 1978

My struggle of the past week ended today when I approached my commanding officer at the naval air station and told him that I had not attended the neurology meeting in California. I did not offer any explanation. I simply told him that once I arrived there I decided not to attend the meetings and that I would return the advanced travel funding I had received. As he sat behind his massive desk, his face sagged. His mouth opened and he started to speak but no words came. Finally, he removed his large gold-rimmed glasses and began cleaning them, even though they were perfectly clean, and said, "I have never had such a thing happen before. I must say I'm touched by your intellectual honesty." He didn't scold. He said the money could be returned and that my authorized time on orders would be changed to leave time.

After I returned the money I still felt somewhat shaken and a little embarrassed. I needed a few minutes to myself so I went to the small chapel where Pat had held his bible classes. I could not collect my thoughts to pray in any meaningful way. I did not even feel particularly soothed. My soul was restless. There was only silence.

I stared at Jesus on the cross and began to feel that my place was to stand there, at his feet. He needs someone to be with him. That someone is going to be me. My place in this great mystery, which Pat has often talked about, is to be with Jesus.

I told Gretchen about what I had gone through today and she said that she admired my courage. I am not sure it was courage. I believe that God has reached out and touched me, and in the process I am going through some sort of internal change. When I think about what I did today, frightened and anxious, even if I had been sent to the brig, my soul would have been at peace.

However, my professional state of mind is far from being at peace. Being a psychiatrist as well as a neurologist with all these feelings makes me feel prepsychotic. Some of my thoughts don't seem to make sense, but in other ways they make perfect sense. I want to be at peace but feel in turmoil. People are probably going to think I am some sort of religious nut.

Wednesday evening, May 3, 1978

My experience of God has gone to my head. Today on rounds I went to see Mr. Carson who was admitted to the hospital two weeks ago because of weakness in his legs. He has had an ascending paralysis of the lower extremities and it is beginning to involve his upper extremities. He is giant of a man and when he is on his feet he is like a great, swaying redwood tree. He fell once and the whole ward shook.

He is still deteriorating and has a polyneuropathy, which is not uncommon for a neurologist to deal with. His tendon reflexes are still absent and he has some tingling in his feet. I tried to "heal" him today. I wiggled his big toe back and forth and asked him whether it was moving up or down. Until today he had not been able to feel the movement much at all.

Today as I wiggled his toe up and down, I prayed for sensation and strength to return. He started to describe accurately which way

I moved his toe and I set myself for a dramatic spiritual miracle. Then he said, "You know I don't know what you're doing down there. I can't feel a damm thing and I think you're wearing my toe out." I was crushed. I wasn't asking for God's help—I was trying to be God—to be special, powerful, and praised for what I had done. I am a fool.

Saturday morning, May 6, 1978

Last night Pat invited Gretchen and me to attend a charismatic prayer meeting. I asked him what *charismatic* means and he said the best way for me to find out was to go to the meeting. With what I thought was thinly-disguised distaste, he said he was not charismatic. "Why are you going then?" "I want to be open to what is happening in the Church." So off we went.

He had apparently been urged to attend by many of his navy chapel flock because as we walked in the door he was immediately surrounded by the friendliest group of people I have ever seen. Some of the emotionalism seemed to border on sickeningly sweet mush. Gretchen became defensive as soon as we walked in because we were approached by a young man who asked us if we had received the Holy Spirit. Gretchen turned to me and I looked around, wondering if I had missed something. Finally, I said, "No, I don't think I have." He shook his head sadly and walked away, saying he would pray for me. I tried to drift away from the crowd to look at some books on display. The women behind the tables reminded me of the "flower children" I had seen when I was going through psychiatry training in the San Francisco Bay area. They had that same far-away look on their faces, clearly living in a state of mind different from mine. They were all very kind, however, and seemed sincere.

The meeting began with some pleasant songs. A few men and women appeared a bit emotional, holding their arms high in the air and occasionally mumbling "glory." The guest speaker was an abbot from an obscure monastery in the Midwest, a rotund Santa Claus of a man who reminded me of a traveling salesman. He gave a reasonable talk, centered on returning the Gospels to the people. Then he drifted into the subject of "inner healing," which stirred the group to an even higher pitch. When he finished speaking the group spontaneously broke into song and another hail of glories and alleluias. I wanted to crawl under my chair.

Another talk was given by a young woman with a puppy-dog look of joy on her face who told of her encounter with God. She had been reared Catholic, going to church and Catholic school "without ever knowing our Lord." The audience responded with an "Amen!" She now felt she should share her encounter with everyone and proceeded to present her story so overdramatically that it turned me off. Her words were accentuated by an occasional breathless "Praise the Lord." A few seats away from us a seedy-looking fellow, grasping a frayed Bible in his hands and shaking it, kept ejaculating, "glory, glory." At one point Pat leaned over to me and whispered, "I wish that damn fool would shut his mouth." About the same time someone behind us started to mumble words that I couldn't understand. I glanced around to see a young woman with her arms up in the air, mumbling incoherently. I turned to Gretchen and said I thought the woman was having a temporal lobe seizure. She and Pat began to laugh and we decided it was time to leave.

Sunday evening, May 7, 1978

I went to church this morning out of curiosity. It seems like the first step if I want to grow and learn more. I think I can learn from Pat. I need him to continue my journey.

It amused me to watch the people in church and compare them to those at the charismatic prayer meeting. This group was much less keyed up and emotional; in fact, there seemed to be very little expression of feelings. People did a great deal of standing up, sitting down, unenthusiastic singing, kneeling, and lining up for a tiny wafer of bread. I felt extremely awkward sitting there with all the movement and song around me. I didn't understand what was going on and felt that the last thing in the world I could do was kneel.

After church I practically ran to my car to return to the relative security of my hospital rounds. At least I can understand patients. Or that's what I thought, until I arrived.

The first patient I saw was Mr. Johnson, a thirty-year-old man dying from severe muscular dystrophy. He was slipping away because his respiratory muscles were becoming too weak for him to breathe. I felt hopelessly overwhelmed when I looked at him. He was semi-comatose, his face was extremely drawn, and his tongue was partly protruding between dusky lips. His young wife sat beside him holding his hand, which had an IV dripping into it. There must have been twenty other people surrounding the bed or hovering around the doorway. I removed everyone from the room except for his wife, and I talked to her for a few moments, explaining the poor prognosis for her husband. A tear began to form in the corner of her eye as I told her he could die within hours or a few days. I then spoke with the entire family who were relieved that he "wasn't suffering" any more. The family appeared to be Catholic; several were clutching rosary beads of various colors and someone had placed two medals of saints around Mr. Johnson's neck.

As I made rounds on the other patients my thoughts kept drifting back to Mr. Johnson, his wife, and their five-year-old son. Before I saw my last four patients I paused in the stairwell where it was quiet and asked God if there was anything else I could do. I immediately had the thought, "You can give yourself up." At first I thought my fantasies had simply run wild, and then I felt that my thought was absurd. Nothing else happened. I felt very free to do whatever I wanted, but I also felt that if I went back to Johnson's bedside I might very well have to give myself up. I thought of dying, somehow, in his place. I didn't like the idea but also felt that if this was God's will, that I could and would do it. I experienced a tremendous amount of trust and I knew at that moment that I would return after rounds to see Mr. Johnson again. I started thinking about Gretchen and my children in California and of never seeing them again. I thought of going down to the lobby to see Gretchen, where she was waiting for me, before I went back to see Mr. Johnson. I believe I was actually preparing to die.

When I returned to his room he didn't look much different. His mother and sister were with him while the rest of the family waited outside. I touched his shoulder and waited. I thought he might wake up and I might get a chest pain. Nothing happened. Then his mother looked up at me with her aging, deep blue eyes and said, "We are ready for this, but it was nice of you to come back. Thank you." I began to feel better then and experienced a sense of peace.

First steps

I told Gretchen about what had happened, not really understanding all of it. She told me I had indeed "given myself up," but emotionally rather than physically. When I returned to Johnson's bedside and his family—something that I found very difficult to do, facing my helplessness again and possibly my own death—I was probably identifying with him because of his age and his young wife. I also gave myself up to something that was not tangible, but was nevertheless very real, very trusting, and very loving.

Monday afternoon, May 15, 1978

Yesterday I did not want to go to church when I woke up in the morning. I felt like a slug crawling on the lid of a garbage pail. Gretchen did not say anything to me or urge me to go. She just told me to follow my feelings about it. I decided to go.

I was impressed with Pat's preparations for Mother's Day. He called all the mothers in the church up to the altar to receive a red rose. It was really very touching. After the service I went back into the church and found a rose for Gretchen. I thought she should have one. After all, she is a stepmother to my children in California, which is probably as difficult as being a "regular" mother. I guess I also wanted her to have one because of all that she means to me.

I left the church this time with a nagging feeling, wishing I had not gone. I felt extremely out of place. I was growing aware of my totally empty background in any religious denomination. I feel like an adult misfit. As everyone kneels, I remain sitting. As the people sing, I silently read the words. As they receive communion, I watch, feeling empty, alone, and out of touch. In some ways I hate it, yet I am strangely drawn to it.

Chapter 3
Conflict

Tuesday evening, May 16, 1978

For the first time in my life I have prayed on my knees.

About an hour ago I got into a terrible fight on the phone with my ex-wife. She won't let the children come to stay with Gretchen and me in Florida for the summer, despite our legal agreement to that effect. I rather sharply told her that this constituted a breach in our agreement and I would give her twenty days to cooperate in arranging the trip or I would discontinue the support payments. With that one of the children got back on the line and said, "You made Mommy cry." It irritates me that I am always at fault.

After that session I felt frustrated and drained. I didn't know what to do. I went into my study and paced, thinking, "Maybe I was unreasonable." Then I felt that it was not I but my ex-wife who had been unreasonable. If she had been in the same room I would have thrown the telephone at her. But I decided that reaction wouldn't help anything. So for the first time in my life I settled down on my knees. I bowed my head and prayed for help. Somehow I did not expect an answer and in many ways I did not even know what to say. I found myself saying, "Please forgive my ex-wife. Help her and help the children." I became teary; I wanted to cry. I did not get any help that would directly change matters with my ex-wife, but somehow I had put myself in God's presence by kneeling and asking for help. I think he heard me and the word *Ishmael*, "God has heard," fleetingly passed through my mind again.

Thursday evening, May 18, 1978

Last night I came home from a difficult day at the hospital. My head was still spinning from the day's activities which began with seeing a patient who had suffered a cardiac arrest and was now comatose, probably with brain death. I had had to give the family the grim news and that interview seemed to set a tragic trend for the day: a spinal-cord tumor in a forty-two-year-old man, multiple sclerosis in a twenty-three-year-old nurse. As soon as I walked in the door and saw Gretchen's face I realized the day wasn't over.

My mother had called, letting us know that a storm had been unleashed since I had notified my ex-wife of the breach in our agreement. Her family was irate, threatening that they were "going to get" me, sue me, and so on. I realized the threats were empty ones but they still made me angry and more fatigued. I wished these people would get a lawyer, so they would be forced to hear my side.

I couldn't sleep when I went to bed. I started talking to God. I had difficulty being serious, speaking to the emptiness around me. All of a sudden I felt a message come rushing through me: "Jeremiah 1–12." I didn't know what it meant but I turned the light on and paged through the Bible. I really did not expect to find anyone named Jeremiah. I was expecting my mind to be playing a nasty trick on me to pop my balloon. I found Jeremiah.

At first I did not know what to read, the first lines of chapter one or chapters one through twelve. I felt frustrated. I started chapter one and felt this was the message because the words began to strike me. I interpreted what I read very personally and probably in a way foreign to any biblical scholar, but I felt that it was a personal message:

> ...The word of the Lord came to me thus: Before I formed you in the womb I knew you, before you were born I dedicated you, a prophet to the nations I appointed you. "Ah, Lord God!" I said, "I know not how to speak; I am too young." But the Lord answered

me, Say not, "I am too young." To whomever I send you, you shall go; whatever I command you, you shall speak. Have no fear before them, because I am with you to deliver you, says the Lord. Then the Lord extended his hand and touched my mouth, saying, See I place my words in your mouth! (Jeremiah 1:4-9)

I began to feel that God had been with me long before my conscious recognition. My very first memory began to flood over me. I was a baby tucked in my crib. I began to dream. I saw a lovely woman, dressed completely in white, standing on the balcony of the house. She beckoned to me and I went to her. I remember feeling a great deal of peace and love, and then in an instant the next thirty years passed before my eyes as I returned to the present. Perhaps more is happening to me than this fight with my ex-wife. I don't know how to speak. I don't understand. I feel angry, as though I am in the midst of a riddle.

Friday, May 19, 1978

This morning before I left for work I settled down on my knees again for a few moments in my study. It wasn't very peaceful; our new kitten, Nuisance, was nipping at my heels and meowing. I became aware of my anger again. I wished all of this was not happening or that I could just ignore it. I wasn't looking for God. I don't need God. He is disrupting my life by showing me who I am.

Now I am faced with a decision. I must either enter into this relationship with God or leave him, ignore his invitation. I already know the answer. I can't turn back and that frustrates me even more.

Perhaps it is more difficult for me right now because I am aware that everything must be according to his will. I am faced with this knowledge as I fight with my ex-wife, who also has to have everything her way. What the hell does he want with me anyway?

Sunday, May 28, 1978

An empty week. There is still no solution to the problem of my children's visit. At times I get very angry with my ex-wife but I have found myself frequently praying for her lately as well as for the children. And even though I am angry when I pray, I am sincere.

Last weekend I went to church alone because Gretchen was working at the hosptial. I wasn't feeling terribly enthusiastic when I walked in. I saw people crossing themselves with holy water and genuflecting in the aisles and I had the urge to leave. When I found out that Pat was not doing the service, I did leave. I just couldn't handle it.

Friday, June 2, 1978

Monday evening I was called to the hospital to see a seven-year-old girl who had suddenly gone into a coma following an upper respiratory infection. She had developed some pernicious vomiting and by the time she reached the hospital was unresponsive. She had papilledema, indicating brain swelling. I told the family I thought she had Reyes syndrome and started Mannitol and steroids right away to reduce the swelling. After all the medications were started I looked down at the child and felt very sorry for her. Neatly combed bright blond hair flowed over the pillow, but her fair skin and slim frame were smothered by machines and tubes, breathing for her and nourishing her. I asked God please to help her. I knew I could do nothing more.

Throughout the week she started to improve, slowly at first, with pupils that became sluggishly reactive, a bit of withdrawal to pinprick, and respirations, the breath of life beginning to return. The parents were frequently praying when I came in on rounds and their faith touched me. Silently, I continued to pray for her also.

This morning she was awake. Her parents said, "It's a miracle." The staff on the ward was amazed, and I was also. Her neurological examination this morning showed that she was essentially normal. Her eyes danced with life and her smile was infectious.

I tried to tell her parents (indirectly of course) how much of a role I had played in helping her when she arrived. I wanted some of the credit, although deep inside I felt that I had done nothing to help her recover. In my heart I believe her recovery was in God's hands. As I walked down the hall away from her room and the smiles of her parents, I glanced at the clown pictures on the walls. I apologized to God for my lack of humility and thanked him for helping this little girl. Simultaneously, I felt very close spiritually to those silly clowns, grinning away into the empty air.

Sunday afternoon, June 3, 1978

Last night I went to bed feeling that the last thing in the world I wanted to do was get up in the morning and attend church. The temptation to sleep in was enormous, and the desire to get up at my leisure, go to the beach, and feel the early summer sunshine wash over me was a powerful one. Instead, when Gretchen and I woke up it was cloudy. Gretchen was going to church as always and since the day looked so bad outside I decided I might as well go too. As I write this I have to admit there was a grain of yearning within me to be with Gretchen and also to go to church.

I think this was the first time I actually enjoyed being at church. I felt a closeness and a comfort there. Some of the words from the eucharistic prayer began to touch me:

> Father, you are holy indeed,
> and all creation rightly gives you praise.
> All life, all holiness comes from you
> through your son, Jesus Christ, our Lord,
> by the working of the Holy Spirit.
> From age to age you gather a people to yourself...

As I watched the congregation make their way to communion I admired the faith that I saw in them and I began to feel very small inside.

I also began to have the most peculiar thoughts. The words from the altar were like an invitation. I felt that I was being gathered in by the Father. I wanted to be at the altar, sharing the space with the priest. I wanted to wear the robes and the cross. At times I felt as though Pat were talking to me.

Things are happening too fast. "I am too young...." At times I can't believe what I feel. My presence at the altar would be absurd. I must be a male hysteric.

Tuesday night, June 6, 1978

I just had a great talk with Pat. He spoke of the mass this past Sunday, mentioning that during the eucharist he had felt that he was talking directly to me. He felt awkward about it and said he had asked God why he should be talking to a non-Catholic when his whole flock was there in front of him. A little uneasily, he admitted that he had felt closer to me during the eucharistic prayer than he had to his parishioners. I found this fascinating, since the words had struck me with such intensity.

Pat expressed regret that he could not speak his true feelings and beliefs to his congregation for fear of frightening them or going over their heads. I told him that I see him "living" his spiritual life and that it always shows when he offers mass. I gave him a parallel in my own life. At the hospital when I teach a course about headaches to a group of medical students or nurses, I am practical and I present the basics. On the other hand, when I am teaching physicians we are able to discuss new and experimental treatments and theory. In church Pat is practical and basic, but when he holds a bible class he can teach on a deeper level. He seemed to like that.

After Pat's openness, I told him my fantasy of being at the altar with him. As soon as I said it I felt a bit foolish. I am not even baptized and here I am wanting to be at the altar. I suddenly asked him about baptism. From my reading I had learned that baptism is somehow necessary if one is to pursue a spiritual life. As soon as I mentioned baptism, however, I felt uneasy. I was not sure I wanted to become a Catholic.

Pat did not try to baptize me on the spot, but explained that he likes to baptize people who are struggling with their spiritual life and choosing to follow in Christ's footsteps. I responded, "Pat, that's me." But I felt an odd reluctance on his part. He said I should continue to read about baptism for a while because it is the first of many steps, and I still know very little about the Church. He also suggested that I attend a few Protestant services to experience other ways of worship. The most important thing, he said, is finding what is right for me.

Chapter 4

Falling in love

Friday, June 9, 1978

    The past two evenings I have prayed at my bedside before retiring. It has been peaceful and I have not asked for anything for a change. I have thanked God for giving his love to me, and for Gretchen and Pat. I have prayed again that my ex-wife and my children also receive his guidance. For a few minutes then I have simply sat in silence with my mind open, without a thought coursing through it.
    After my prayer time I have continued my nightly reading. I am currently reading *Christ Among Us,* by Anthony Wilhelm, and as the book mentions bible passages I have been reading some of them.
    There is a raging thunderstorm occurring right now but I am at peace. I feel warm inside, as if I am falling in love.

Thursday morning, June 15, 1978

    A few nights ago I had the most curious dream that has persisted in my memory: I was polishing a glass table with a cloth. There was a smudge which seemed irremovable all over the surface of the glass. At first as I rubbed there was no change, but then the glass began to clear at the edge of the cloth, and I felt the presence of God working through my hand. The entire table began to clear except for the upper left corner. I then woke up and reflected on the dream. I felt that somehow, as God's instrument, I can clear up some of the mystery we face in our faith. But there will always remain an elusive smudge of mystery that can never be removed by human hands or minds.

Since my dream I have continued my journey into faith in the same disorderly fashion. I continue to pray briefly at night and to read the Bible and other books. For the most part my prayers have been quiet; rarely do I utter words aloud. One night I had a terrific headache. I asked for God's help and didn't get it.

Over the weekend my grandparents came to visit and I sat down to play a game of chess with my grandfather. I prayed eagerly for victory but I was soundly defeated five times. Although my trivial wishes were not fulfilled, many of my true desires were. I was pleased that my grandmother was well enough to visit us, that we could share meals together, play card games and chess. These moments brought joy, headache and all.

Friday evening, June 16, 1978

Sometimes I feel that I scream and kick like an infant, wanting everything. But, if I had everything, what would I really have?

Earlier this evening I sat talking with my grandmother and felt a curious sensation that she was talking to me about my future. She told me that my great uncle had developed the pure beeswax candle for the Catholic Church. In the process he had become the only one in our family to convert to Catholicism. This event caused great upheaval in the entire family and when he died his son refused to bury him as a Catholic. What a pity that his son never knew him.

Am I like my great uncle? Am I going to become a Catholic and in the process become a social outcast in my own family? If God is calling me I must follow despite the feelings of my family. I may not offer the light of a candle, but I can offer myself.

Sunday evening, June 18, 1978

I have read several chapters lately on the meaning of the Mass and I still don't understand. I don't understand Christ in the eucharist. I don't understand baptism. How does all this enable us to draw closer to God? My reading says that if we accept these things we will become closer.

Sometimes when I look at Pat during the eucharistic prayer, I feel that I am seeing Jesus—that somehow Jesus really is talking to me, just as he is talking to all the people in the church. But at the same time I feel that I am not one of his flock. I am a man without a church. And what am I writing all this for? It will probably end up in the nearest trash can with my ashes.

Monday evening, June 26, 1978

I prayed for strength and decided to call my ex-wife. I felt as if my insides were about to shake loose. My stomach was in a knot and my hands were so moist I could barely hold the phone. I hate confrontation but I finally realized that I had to talk with her to resolve the current situation with the children. It was our first talk in many months but it was fruitful and now Todd, my seven-year-old son, is on his way here. Brent, my youngest, will be coming in a few weeks. I don't know if God helped me through this step but at least I didn't feel alone.

Tuesday evening, June 27, 1978

For the past few weeks I have continued to read about the Catholic faith and the Church without understanding very well. At the same time my evening prayers have been fitful and fruitless. I have asked for an understanding of the Church and of how Jesus fits into the picture. There has not been an answer. Perhaps being a psychiatrist has made me even more aware of the awesome silence. I wonder if the silence itself is not an answer. If anything, it has made me feel very alone, and it is somehow driving me to the Church, the only place I can go now for my floundering new spiritual life.

Falling in love

There is no question that the Church is beginning to mean more to me. This past Sunday for the first time I did not feel like an outsider. Despite my awkwardness, I felt I was part of the group. Pat gave a beautiful, simple sermon, quoting from a work by C. S. Lewis (an atheist who became a convert). I saw a direct parallel to my own life. He compared our growth in the Church to the domestication of a puppy who must learn the "human" world. He must not chew on pillows, bite, or use the family carpet as a litter box. This process is very difficult, painful at times, and confusing. Often in our spiritual growth there seem to be no answers, few handles to grasp. We wonder whether God hears us or even cares. We are learning the spiritual world, very different from the physical world, a process that is often painful and confusing.

For the eucharist, Pat brought forth bread, freshly baked by the people within the congregation according to early Christian tradition. I was moved to tears. Suddenly I was filled with a rush of feelings about this symbolism. What happened almost two thousand years ago was flooding back to this moment. Jesus, by his life and actions, left us this eucharist:

> Before he was given up for death, a death he freely accepted, he took bread and gave you thanks. He broke the bread, gave it to his disciples and said: Take this, all of you, and eat it: this is my body which will be given up for you.

What a beautiful gift this is, but one not to be forced. In front of me I saw a little boy whose mother was prodding him to kneel. Even with all my feelings I did not kneel, but I know now that someday I will. It's as though my prodding is coming from inside, and, like the little boy, I am still fighting it.

Thursday, June 29, 1978

I called Pat yesterday and told him how I had enjoyed his Sunday service. I shared the feelings I had had about the eucharist. He was winded from his five-mile jog but he said that my words lifted his spirits. He then became serious and asked me to re-read the chapter on baptism in *Christ Among Us*. He said I might want to consider being baptized, but he wanted me to read more, think about it for a couple of weeks, and then we would talk. If it feels right he said he would consider baptizing me during a mass.

I was a bit surprised. I felt both anxious and excited. I still have reservations about becoming a Catholic, yet I do not feel anxious anymore about being baptized as a Christian. I think I would welcome it.

This past Sunday I did feel closer to the Catholic faith, especially the beauty of the eucharist and the scripture readings. I don't know what my problem is with Catholicism. Gretchen is a Catholic and is a beautiful person, sharing her faith in the way she lives her life, caring for patients and giving herself freely. Some of my block must be deeply rooted from seeds planted in my childhood. I remember seeing Catholic children dressed in uniform walking to their own school up the street. They weren't any fun at all—they didn't swear and despite our calling them "snappers" continued to eat fish on Fridays. They wouldn't go the bathroom behind a crop of trees like the other boys in the neighborhood, and any talk of sex was totally prohibited. One foot off that narrow line and they would go straight to hell, according to their parents, who thought everything was improper and evil except going to church. I also remember how my parents said the word *Catholic* as if it were a dirty toilet scat. Even Gretchen's parents are a road block to me, the way they seem to have so little love for their daughter, because she married "a divorced man, with children no less." And I see other Catholics who are incredibly rigid.

In some ways my reservations are small, but they create a turmoil within me. I will do the reading Pat suggested and pray to God for his guidance. Perhaps my view of the Church is distorted. I know there is also beauty there because I feel it in my heart and I see it in the bread and wine.

Monday, July 3, 1978

Gretchen and Todd are not hitting it off. Gretchen wants to love and accept him but she occasionally feels that he is an intrusion and the two of them snap at each other for the slightest reason. I am actually pleased with their relationship and have told them. Their irritation with each other is open and there are subtle signs of true caring. They simply need time; any relationship needs time to develop.

I wish it were as easy for me to hear these words about my own relationship with God. It has been a continuous struggle. If only I could say, "I was converted one day and life became beautiful." At this point I realize that I have been converted and there is a great deal of beauty in those words, but there are so many storms to undergo. Sometimes I feel I am floundering like a beached fish, flopping around looking for the water. I am beginning to love this relationship with God but it is all so puzzling to me.

I have been reading about baptism and the idea is growing on me. I see it as a way to become "immersed" in the spiritual life, paralleling the death and resurrection of Christ, beginning a new life. What bothers me is that I don't see many Catholics living this way. The majority seem to live on a straight and narrow line of rigidity, where instead of many things being "right," they are seen as "wrong." Despite my perception, I want to follow what is in my heart. I yearn to go deeper, to learn more.

Monday, July 10, 1978

Pat and I talked today about baptism. At this point I have no hesitation. To be symbolically born again (resurrected) and join the struggle of Christianity is extremely appealing and I feel ready. Yet I still hesitate about entering the Catholic Church. Pat told me that I need to choose a church that most comfortably fits my way of worship and self-expression, one in which I can feel comfortable participating in the struggle to know God. Pat reacts strongly to many of his people who do not practice their faith but ask him to baptize their babies so the infants will not go to "limbo." He has caused a great stir by refusing to perform these baptisms because he feels that the parents must set an example for their children. Baptism isn't magic; it is an initiation into the Christian community.

I cannot help feeling that God has led me to where I am now, and that I should simply continue in this direction. I feel that I have clearly been led to this Church, as I have been to Pat and his teaching, in Jesus' footsteps. Nor can I overlook Gretchen who tenderly and lovingly has always been at my side, never pushing but always supporting. If she had pushed me, I know I would have rebelled and gone in the opposite direction. She has given me the freedom to grow and to learn, to be myself.

Wednesday, July 12, 1978

I attended mass at noon yesterday in the small chapel. A somewhat comical but serious priest named Father Dawson presided.

I felt extremely uneasy. As much as I hesitate to say it I felt embarrassed being there. I wanted to sneak in without being seen. I could not get into it; I felt clinical. There were nine people there and several times all rose to their feet in unison as if on cue, but I never knew what the cue was so I was always a half count behind. On one occasion I didn't see them stand and bolted to my feet, just as they were all beginning to sit again. I must have looked like an idiotic jack-in-the-box.

Father Dawson spoke quickly and the group responded like well-trained parrots. My mouth opened and closed silently like that of a stranded fish. The people walked up to the altar where Father Dawson distributed communion. I remained in my seat, alone, wondering why in the world I had to come to a daily mass. When the others crossed themselves I felt it was absurd. I just could not do it. On the way out they dipped their fingers in a bowl of water near the door and blessed themselves again. I hurried past the bowl and out into the hot afternoon sunshine, convinced that I could never become a Catholic. The behavior of Catholics at times is incomprehensible to me. I can never see myself learning such rituals. Perhaps I am retreating to my familiar background of believing God is a neurosis, a way for people to face their inevitable death with some degree of comfort.

I feel that I am being forced to learn, but no one is forcing me. As Father Dawson said during mass, faith is something for which we will not be billed; we are free to choose it.

I crawled into Pat's office after mass and moaned and groaned that I didn't fit into this madness. We talked for an hour and I finally started to settle down. He explained that dipping into the holy water was symbolic of dipping into the mystery of all that water represents: it is necessary for our life; it is the very substance of our bodies; and it can be deadly. He also explained the sign of the cross as the vertical line representing our attempt to reach the spiritually infinite and intangible God, linked with the horizontal, our human earthly life. In our lives we relate vertically to God and horizontally to each other, but the process is all one. We must approach the mystery in a straightforward, tangible (horizontal) way. We can only relate to God in our human ways. Pat quoted Paul, saying, "My mind says this, but my body does this." He said the sign of the cross was also a secret sign of greeting for the early Christians who were in constant danger of being fed to the lions.

Pat reminded me again of my youth in the Church. I should expect to be uneasy with the rituals. I need to think of being a Christian first, and a Catholic second.

Thursday, July 13, 1978

I attended Pat's daily mass today and again became rooted to my seat and totally discouraged. I could not concentrate on his message. There were only six people present. Five went to the altar for communion and I remained in my pew, desolate. I ached inside and kept my head bowed because inside I was thinking, "I can't do this. This isn't for me." I felt sorry for myself. If spiritual growth is like a seed, I fear mine will never sprout.

After mass I walked with Pat back to his office, my face sagging. We talked for a very long hour. I told him I was going through an extremely painful period and he said things may get even worse. I said I felt like a seed growing alone deep in the cold, dark soil with no way out. As I reach for the sunlight I hit a rock, am chewed on by a snail, and unloaded on by a dog.

Pat reflected on a poem, *The Hound of Heaven,* saying how God is sometimes like a hound who pursues us, even when we try to flee him. That image fit perfectly. I have been trying to run away from God, and I can't get away. In my heart I know I am in love.

Chapter 5

Bread and wine

Monday, July 17, 1978

Yesterday I accepted the bread and the wine.

Pat began his homily about the Church. It is neither the great white building in which we were all sitting, nor is it the pope or the hierarchy of the Church. *We are* the Church. We are the body of Christ and we celebrate with a meal of bread and wine. We offer Jesus back to the Father in the form of bread and wine, the perfect sacrifice.

It all started to come alive for me. On that last night when Jesus was betrayed, the night prior to his death, he spoke to his Apostles of the bread and wine. It was not a joyous occasion. The room was filled with a dreadful anxiety and perhaps even gloom. Jesus was leaving them and they were overwhelmed with uncertainty and emptiness. There are times when we all reach out and find only emptiness and uncertainty. But he left us the bread and wine, his body and blood. "Take this, all of you, and eat it: this is my body which will be given up for you. Do this in remembrance of me."

I realized then that I have been sitting and waiting for things to be right for me to take the bread and wine. All of a sudden I knew that there wasn't going to be a right time. My time was now. I stood up and turned to Gretchen and said simply, "It's time." She was speechless. I could read her expression: "You can't do this; you aren't baptized!" I felt it didn't matter. Jesus never witheld himself from those who approached him in love and sincerity. I knew I was struggling, but I wanted to share in this meal. My knees felt watery. I accepted the bread from Pat and then drank from the cup. There was no heavenly music and angels didn't start singing, even though the choir music was drifting softly in the air.

My timing was not perfect. I had been waiting for the perfect time to accept the eucharist. I had been waiting for God to tap me on the shoulder and say, "It's your turn." Then I realized that I have to reach out too. Yesterday, I reached out to become part of the mystery, instead of simply watching it.

I accepted the bread in my hand and carried it for a moment to think about what I was doing. When I placed it in my mouth I thought it was tasteless, like cardboard. Was it as tasteless for the Apostles? That last night was an uncomfortable one. Perhaps they asked themselves, "What in the world is all this about? Who is this man? What is he saying?" But they took the bread, and I did too. When I returned to my pew, I knelt down for the first time. I did not feel awkward.

As Gretchen and I walked from the church, enjoying the warmth of the summer sun and holding hands, she turned to me and said, "You know, I think your seed may have just grown its first sprout. I love you." And I love her.

Tuesday, July 18, 1978

Today my mother arrived for a ten-day visit and brought Brent, my youngest son, who will stay for two weeks with Todd. Our house is a bit packed at the moment but it's good to have the boys here. My mother's presence is another story. She is a night owl type who likes to sleep until noon, and that isn't the way things are at our house.

Wednesday, July 26, 1978

I have been wanting to write for over a week but I've been bombarded with consults all over the hospital. The pace has been maddening. Patients have come in with seizures, headaches, strokes, and other peculiar ailments that in most cases have turned out to be alcoholism. I have been so busy that all my tenderness and empathy have dried up.

Yesterday morning I awoke to a thunderstorm that made the house seem dark even with the lights on. As I looked at myself in the mirror, my nagging doubts returned. I told myself that my interest in spiritual life is crazy. I tried to pray but my pager went off for me to call the intensive care unit. Lord, why do you want a doctor?

Thursday, July 27, 1978

Feeling like a mindless child, I attended Pat's noon mass. I boldly attempted to say the Lord's prayer, got half way through and had to mumble the rest because I didn't know the words. I approached the altar with the others and accepted the bread and wine again. After my sip of wine, instead of walking back to the pew and kneeling, I stepped in front of the altar and just stood there. I must have looked like some sort of nut, but I didn't feel like one. I was part of the group; I am new and I am going to fumble with some of the routine for a while.

After mass, Pat and I met and had a good talk. I told him how the words of the eucharistic prayer seem alive to me. They strike my ears with a deeper meaning every time I hear them. Pat then reminded me to attend some Protestant services for my growth.

Saturday evening, July 29, 1978

This morning I decided impulsively to send Todd and Brent home with my mother. As hard as it is to admit, I am tired of all our visitors on top of my work. I want some peace. I could also save money by sending them with my mother—my excuse for not telling my ex-wife the truth. I called and told her I was sending them home. She cried and screamed at me for making a commitment to keep the boys for two weeks (true), and I responded with a cool callousness that since I was paying the bill I could do whatever I damn well pleased. The experience was turning my stomach upside down and fraying my nerves so I told her I would think about it and call her back. I drove to the beach like a maniac and buried my anxiety in the warm sand, trying to figure out what was right. I was compromising her plans again. She can change her plans but I never can.

I came home to pray my longest prayer, asking God to solve my petty problem. Silence. Then I felt truly helpless and didn't know what to say. I thought of the children. In all the turmoil of the morning I had forgotten them. Outside my study, I heard my mother tell Gretchen she really didn't want the boys to go home with her. Then anger welled up and I felt like a babysitter. Somehow I sensed that God was telling me he is not going to be my babysitter. Finally, I opened myself: "If it is your will, please help us resolve this matter in the children's best interests." Crystallizing in my consciousness came the answer: "Keep them."

I called my ex-wife and told her I would keep Todd and Brent, adding that I would charge her for the nursery and the difference in plane fare. She flew into a rage, screaming that I was blackmailing her. I got angry, stated through gritted teeth that I would send them back in two weeks, and hung up.

Two hours later she called back. Her tone had changed and I had also mellowed during the interim. I had started to feel foolish, realizing that I had promised to keep the children two to three weeks and I had impulsively unloaded on her. She said the hassle was not worth it to her and if I wanted to send the boys back now, to go ahead. I apologized for my behavior and agreed to keep them. We parted in peace. As I hung up the phone, I was suddenly filled with the warmth of human compassion. In this case my ex-wife had reached out in peace to me. I was sure we were both experiencing God's peace.

Sunday evening, July 30, 1978

This morning I got up with the sun to make rounds early and get to the Protestant service at the naval air station by 10:30 a.m. As I settled into my seat and listened to the blaring of the pipe organ I heard another blaring—my pager. I was told to call the emergency room. I missed fifteen minutes trying to find a telephone and advising the residents on how to handle a seizure.

Returning, I opened the door to hear the Presbyterian chaplain proclaim loudly, "We must practice the fear of God in order to know wisdom." That statement turned me off. I personally feel awe, but not fear. However, as he continued, he said that fear develops as we become aware of the awesomeness of God. Thinking of the awesomeness of God gave me a twinge of fear, but I still don't agree that we must "live in fear of his mighty hand." The sermon turned out to be interesting because he talked about how to pray: be specific; ask for wisdom and ask what is God's will. The sermon was followed by readings and hymns that reflected the same message.

I could not find fault with the Protestant service but there was something missing for me—the bread. Behind the altar the large gold cross stood out boldly against scarlet curtains—empty; Jesus was not on it. Despite the words of praise, songs, and the loud trumpeting of the pipe organ, the crowded church felt empty in some way. Jesus—and the bread he left for us—were not there. I cannot speak for the others but for me there seemed to be only silence.

After church, my mother wanted to go to the beach and swim one more time before she left. Because of the frequent thunderstorms the surf was pounding against the sand in a storm of its own. My poor mother was helpless in it, standing ankle deep in the swirling white water waiting for it to change. I felt sorry for her because she had been waiting for days to swim. Todd and Brent didn't mind at all—they frolicked in the rough waves, giggling and squealing as they were thrown from their feet and washed up on the shore. I was glad I hadn't sent them home. And I prayed for the surf to calm down for my mother.

Just then a young man came walking along the shore, passing near my mother. She turned and asked him if there was a "drop-off" out there. He replied that there wasn't, but that it was very rough. Then his words were lost in the roar of the pounding waves as he turned and pointed in a direction behind us. It suddenly hit me—the bay! My mother could swim in the bay. I couldn't believe it. I pulled Todd and Brent from the surf, called to my mother, and we went to the bay where she had her swim.

As I sat on the sand watching the three of them play and splash in the water, I wondered about God. I had just witnessed how God uses us as instruments. I was also impressed that it would never have occurred to me that the young man was pointing to the bay had I not just prayed. I was filled with both awe and doubt. I had received an answer but not what I had asked. I wanted the storm to stop so my mother could swim, but God's way was simply to say, "If you move, your mother can swim. I am not going to stop the whole storm for you." It is like any relationship. We must take an active part—not just sit there wishing for the storms to be taken away, or the other one to change. We too must be open to change, and we must listen.

Tuesday, August 1, 1978

I am very tired today. Yesterday I had to get up at 5:30 a.m. to do my rounds in time to work in the adult primary care clinic at the hospital. I worked until 10:00 p.m., treating all the things a neurologist abhors: runny noses, sore throats, pelvic pain, constipation. I found myself praying to see someone in a coma, or with a headache. I also covered psychiatry last night because the psychiatrist was called out of town and I was suddenly the only psychiatrist at the hospital. Sometimes I think I wear too many hats. Yet there is another hat I want to wear. I want to be part of the Church. I want to stand with Christ at his altar.

Monday, August 7, 1978

Yesterday our pope died. Somehow, even though I am not a Catholic, I feel Pope Paul VI was indeed "our" pope. He was for all of us, as God is. We will miss him, but we will continue to grow in his spirit.

I managed to attend another Protestant service yesterday. A Congregational minister was the guest speaker at the navy chapel. There was a kind of glow about him as he spoke, revealing his closeness to spiritual life and his abundant knowledge. However, he spoke a bit too long and my body became somewhat restless. My thoughts wandered to Todd and Brent in the chapel nursery listening to the pipe organ. I wondered what their feelings were about all this. They have had little exposure to church. Since being here they have had many questions about Jesus and God. They were understandably confused by my awkward explanations. Then I realized that I am not far from where they stand, at ages five and seven. The only thing they seemed to grasp was the concept that God is like the wind; he never dies and is always there. We cannot see him, but we can feel his presence. In some ways I feel that I am leading them as he is leading me, a few steps at a time—a taste to whet their appetites and bring questions to their minds.

I felt at ease at the Protestant service. I even sang with the people around me, something I have never done in church. I could continue in the Protestant church, but I feel that I would be missing my own personal calling somehow. The Catholic Church needs help. What on earth (or in heaven) I will ever bring to it I have no idea. But that is to be my direction. I feel an active struggle in the Catholic Church, a spiritual struggle, whereas I felt a momentary peace in the Protestant group. I sense there will be difficult times ahead for me. I think it would be easier for me to become a Protestant, but I would simply be burying my head in the sand and living as I did in my first marriage, saying everything was fine, knowing in my heart that something was not right, and living on a falsely even keel. Now it seems that the times on an even keel are rare. I plunge into confusion, loneliness, and more love than I have ever known before.

I received a card from Pat a few days ago that warmed my heart and raised my spirits. He is on retreat. He wrote: "The center of our retreat has been the eucharist. It has enriched my spirituality. Growth in the spirit happens every day. I remember you daily at the table of God. Give my best to Gretchen and the boys. See you when I get home. In his spirit, Pat."

The boys are going home today. Three weeks pass so rapidly. We had a good visit and I am sorry to see it end, but I know it must for now. I really love them.

Chapter 6

A calling

Monday, August 14, 1978

Father Dawson very nearly pierced my heart with his parting words at mass yesterday, and I don't think he even realized what he said.

I enjoyed getting back to mass. Father Dawson centered his homily on remembering Pope Paul VI and praying for the cardinals to be guided by the Holy Spirit in their election of a new pope. For a change, I had no difficulty at all with my prayer. More than ever before I stopped thinking about everything and simply participated. I even sang.

Father Dawson quoted words from Pope Paul VI, saying, "Any day is a good day to be born and a good day to die. I always think of that other shore and submit to the will of the Lord, whether he decides to keep me here or call me to him." He then asked an intriguing question: "What if we were called to our death this instant? How would we respond? Would we ask God for a few minutes, an hour? Would we ask for time to say our goodbyes and get our things in order, or would we be ready to go at a moment's notice?" I am afraid most of us do not have our bags packed, even though we would like to say we are ready. Very few of us live our daily lives as we do during that hour on Sunday. I know I don't. Days slip by when I forget God, or choose to squander my time.

After communion we prayed in silence. Father Dawson slipped down from the altar and sat in the pew immediately in front of me and bowed his head. I am glad he was with us for a few moments. It was when he stood up and began to speak again that his words nearly bolted me to the pew. I felt as if he were talking directly to me. He said, "I like coming out here with the people from time to time. It reminds me of when I was a deacon. It is very significant that every priest and bishop is first ordained a deacon. It remains a basic element in our life, that we should be the least of our brothers, for the good of all." He looked down at me and said, "A deacon comes from the people, remains with the people, and works for the people." He then turned and walked back up to the altar. My head was in an absolute spin. I believe God is calling me to yet another shore. This incident seemed to crystallize my thoughts about being at the altar. I guess time and the will of God will tell.

Tuesday, August 15, 1978

Today I was again very aware of "timing." In between patients this morning, I was sitting at my desk recalling what Father Dawson had said about the deacon. As I began to consider what it might be like to pursue training as a deacon, my phone buzzed and the corpsman at the desk asked me if I recognized a certain phone number in California. I did not. He explained that it was an unauthorized call dialed from one of our clinic telephones.

After hanging up I remembered a hurried phone call I had made to a bank in California several months before. I had not informed anybody about it. Just a few moments ago I would not have had a second thought about making an unauthorized phone call. No one would ever discover that it was mine. In some ways it still didn't bother me.

Then the timing of the incident struck me. There I was, thinking about how I would like to be a deacon in the Church, and live my daily life honestly as a Christian, and at the same time I was being tempted to lie about an almost insignificant act. It came down to a simple decision: if I really want to continue on this journey toward God, I must live as his son did and not merely give lip service.

A calling

I was uneasy then about admitting that I had made the unauthorized phone call. I felt like an idiot, but the timing haunted me. I decided I had to do it. Suddenly, I felt the words flow through me: "You shall be a deacon." It is as if I had been given a bit of a test, and I had passed. I no longer felt uneasy about admitting to the telephone call.

So I calmly acknowledged my misdeed, but the lanky staff civil engineer after searching through the files for several minutes could not find any record of the call! The number he had and the phone number in the clinic were not mine. He said, "Forget it." But I don't think I ever will.

Thursday, August 17, 1978

Pat doesn't feel that I should become a deacon. He thinks I should wait.

We had an extremely difficult talk yesterday. It began after the noon mass when I met two candidates to the diaconate. One has already completed a year of training in the Diocese of Pensacola-Tallahassee and the other is starting this September. They are both several years my senior. I started to get excited talking with them about the program—learning about scripture and Church history, and concentrating on prayer. I also felt something else, a sort of kinship that I have never known. With them I was not a military officer and a physician but another human being. I also felt that we were heading in the same direction, not in competition but as students of life in the spirit.

I saw an opportunity before me, along with some difficulties. The new diaconate class begins in just four weeks, and I have not even been baptized yet. I was suddenly eager to get on with baptism so I could be considered for the class.

My eagerness crashed in Pat's office. We talked about my being baptized and confirmed on August 27. He informed me rather seriously that there are certain responsibilities of which I must be aware: I am expected to attend church regularly and make a confession at least once each year. I tried to joke with him, saying I confess to him every day. The responsibilities didn't bother me. I told him I wanted to become a deacon. There was a rather long silence.

He doesn't think I'm ready. He thinks I should wait. There would be too many "administrative difficulties," such as the fact that I will be baptized in the military ordinariate, which does not ordain deacons. But I don't care about administrative difficulties. I want to join the program here in Pensacola where I am planning to stay after I am out of the navy. Pat looked sad, and said he didn't want to see me start into it and burn out; it reminded him of when he originally entered the seminary and had to leave for four months because he burned out.

There was more to our conversation than just words. There was a tremendous outpouring of emotion. I sensed that I was taking my first step away from him as my teacher, the one who had guided me into the Church. I felt that I was moving away from him by being baptized and wanting to enter the diaconate program. At one point my eyes started to fill, as I thought of what I was about to do and how I will miss him when he leaves in eight months. I also thought he was being a bit overprotective. I am going to have to go out into the Church and do my thing, whatever it is. We both ended up feeling wrung out and confused. At the end of our meeting he suggested that we pray for a moment. He asked for God's help and guidance for both of us, whatever his will.

When I got home I sat wondering whether I should even be baptized. A strong desire to enter the diaconate program kept washing over me, then minutes later I would step back and wonder whether it would be a mistake. I don't think I am simply having "an affair of the spirit" that will burn out in a few months. I think it is a way to become more deeply involved and I feel that I am really being called to something.

I don't know what to do. I guess the best thing is to pray and wait to see what develops. At the moment I have to prepare a lecture on head trauma for the family-practice residents, so my lay reality beckons.

Friday evening, August 18, 1978

Lord, where are you taking me? Everything was so simple just a few hours ago. All I wanted to do was take the afternoon off. I came home to mow the lawn and Gretchen told me to call Pat because he

A calling

was looking everywhere for me—"something about the diaconate program."

The something turned out to be the discovery that the first class of the current year is starting tomorrow. My mind started racing as soon as I heard. I felt overwhelmed—this is too fast for me. Pat told me one of the candidates has invited me to go with him tomorrow morning. He is leaving at 7:00 a.m. That means if I go I have to get up at 5:30 a.m. I told Pat I didn't know what to do. He said he had talked with Father Fausto, the director of the program, who has also invited me to come and observe. He gave me Father Fausto's telephone number and said, "Russ, let God help you decide; he'll show you which way to go."

I didn't think even God could help me with this one; it was almost more than I could handle. I went out and mowed the lawn absentmindedly, mulling the idea over and over. One of the biggest (and most absurd) road blocks was the idea of getting up at 5:30. I love sleeping in on Saturday morning with Gretchen. I wait all week for it. My stomach began to tie into a knot. I decided to call Father Fausto.

When Father Fausto answered, a horde of butterflies started fluttering in my stomach. I mumbled a clumsy introduction then and had some trouble understanding him because of his thick Italian accent. All I could make out for certain was an air of friendliness and the word *beautiful*, which he said several times and, "God love you." I think he suggested I come and observe.

I still don't know what to do. I feel an urge, however, to set my alarm clock for 5:30 a.m.

Saturday evening, August 19, 1978

I couldn't believe it when I dragged myself out of bed in the early morning darkness. I had spent an absolutely hideous night tossing and turning, and as I pulled out of the driveway I felt like one possessed.

The sun was just beginning to touch the day when I parked in front of a very large house. A small group of men were milling around in the driveway, embracing and calling one another "brother." I mumbled an uncharitable word under my breath and told myself to turn around now. Don't get involved with these people; get out quickly. But my damn feet kept walking. The men treated me like an arriving cactus plant and I didn't receive a single hug. (I can't say I deserved one.) Bill Harris, a large bear of a man, and his lovely wife tried to make me feel comfortable. He is a recently retired navy chief who has since let his hair and beard grow. He wore a large wooden cross around his neck and is beginning his second year in the diaconate training program. He is also attending the university, planning to teach emotionally disturbed children.

When I climbed into the van for the two-hour ride to Panama City, I felt like a trapped sardine. I didn't want to talk to anyone. At one point I prayed that the van would break down so that I could walk home. We finally arrived at the motel and as the meeting room filled, there was more hugging and kissing. I found a seat in the back, in a corner.

We were given an outline of the course. Three years of monthly weekend meetings for fourteen hours of instruction and times for prayer, fellowship, and mass. Two of the weekends would be devoted to spiritual retreats and there would be interim monthly meetings to share problems and so on.

Out of nowhere a gaunt, chain-smoking young priest named Father Reardon started pacing at the front of the room. With great care he wrote the words *revelation* and *inspiration* in large letters on his overhead projector and then looked up at us with a wry smile on his serious, scholarly face. He began to address us in a loud lecture hall voice. (He must give powerful sermons.) He was going to give us an introduction to scripture and with just a hint of that smile, he said, "I am also about to shake your faith."

His lecture was powerful, probing, and captivating, the introduction to a series of lectures that would be six hours each monthly weekend for the next year. After one hour had passed, I wanted to come back.

His teaching on revelation came mainly from the documents of Vatican II. Divine revelation is the message of God, both inside and outside the Bible. It is the way God reveals himself through scripture and tradition. We can have a personal self-revelation of God, and by divine acts, see how he reveals himself, not all at once, but step by step. Revelation is not homogeneous; sometimes God speaks and sometimes he is silent. I was so fascinated I was getting goose bumps on my arms.

A calling

Father Reardon went on to discuss inspiration, and how we believe the Bible is "the written word of God." The Holy Spirit inspires the author to write and preserves revelation from error. (However, the inspired word is not dictation.) He then explained how the Bible must be interpreted in relation to the style of the author and what the author was intending to say. For instance, some books of the Bible were probably intended to give a message through fiction rather than historical fact. With that, some of the men trained as Catholics thirty or more years ago started to stir uncomfortably and a few arguments ensued. A couple of the men chose to believe the Bible literally. I wasn't shaken at all since I had no preconceived notions.

Father Reardon calmly lit another cigarette and took a few steps away from his projector. "You men, if you are going to pursue training as ministers in the Church, had better learn to open your minds. What I am saying is the teaching of the Church. It is not the Baltimore Catechism, and it is certainly not what you learned as youngsters twenty-five years ago. If you choose to cling to literal interpretation, you won't grow and you won't be able to teach what is in the Bible." The room was silent.

We ate lunch together, the group radiating a spiritual warmth. The food prepared by the wives appeared magically. Even though I still did not feel that I was part of the gathering I appreciated being there. I thought if there was a Holy Spirit he was within this group of people from every walk of life, with ages ranging from thirty-two (me) to approximately seventy.

By chance I sat next to Peter Weiss, a compulsive, argumentative man with a sharply chiseled face, who soon realized I knew nothing at all about the Church and attempted to explain basic Catholic doctrine to me. He used to be a university professor of romantic languages, but now sells real estate in order to devote more time to the Church. The only time he smiled was when he was arguing. At times during the lecture he had adamantly challenged Father Reardon, but it was clear the priest was always one step ahead of him, whether it had to do with translation or interpretation.

I finally extracted myself from Peter's presence and found another physician. I gravitated to him for the rest of the lunch hour for security. Bob Saxer was a kind, well-dressed, red-bearded pediatrician who, among other things, offered me a job in his clinic. I enjoyed talking with him. At one point he said, "I try to find God in my daily life. In my practice of medicine there are times that I know God exists simply by watching a baby after birth."

After lunch, I met with Father Fausto for a half-hour interview. Fausto, a middle-aged, short, thick man with a wave of lustrous black hair falling carelessly over a high forehead, was glowing with life's spirit. His eyes were dark, smiling, eloquent. He reminded me of an Italian Santa Claus. I was immediately at ease with this man and found myself smiling back at him. When I reached out to shake his hand, he extended his arms and gave me a hug, saying, "God love you." Ordinarily this approach would have turned me off, but his embrace did not bother me at all. He apologized, "Forgive me, it is my Italian blood. I love to hug people, especially the women."

He listened attentively as I told him that I didn't know why I had come. All of this seemed to be happening so fast I could hardly believe I was there at all. Yet I felt very strongly that there must be some reason; I was enjoying it and I wanted to stay. Fausto informed me that the current class was actually filled and that he had had to turn down several good applicants, advising them to apply again next year. He said that since I had not been baptized this approach might be my best course. But then he bent his head and I heard him mumble something like, "Ah, *mama mia*, come follow me." When he looked up he brushed his hair back and said, "I think you are here for a reason too; you will have a difficult time. You are young. You are very new in the Church. You will have problems that many of the other candidates will not have because much of the Church is second nature to them. You will not only have to learn all we are teaching, you will have to learn what it is to be a Catholic. I would like you to join us. For now, don't think about ordination; just think about learning." I smiled and felt a glow inside. I began to soar, buoyant with love and excitement. Father Fausto must have seen this in my face, because he said, "God is wonderful, isn't he? I told you of all the problems you will face but you will also know something more. You will feel more love and joy in your life than you have ever felt before." Throughout the rest of the afternoon I had great difficulty planting my feet firmly back on the earth.

When I returned home I found Gretchen and Pat pacing like expectant parents, waiting to hear about my day. At first I could only hug them both, then I blurted out the day's happenings. I saw them exchange a look that said, "My God, he's really done it." Pat was cautious and continued to pace, saying, "Well, just take one class at a time. See how it goes." This evening I said grace before dinner for the first time: "Thank you, Lord, for bringing us together and to where we are now. Thank you for the friendship and the love that we have for one another." I am so happy to have Pat and Gretchen in my life. They both mean so much to me.

Sunday, August 20, 1978

I don't think I know what it's like to be touched by the Spirit, but I can't help feeling that I have experienced it. I don't know what it is, or why I am where I am, but I trust God's will. Even now, though, I am aware of some doubts. I may be overwhelmed after two months and drop out, but I feel as if I am being drawn like iron filings to a magnet, to grow more in the spiritual life, perhaps to become a teacher and a servant. There are times I feel that I am not the type to be a servant to others; I am too self-centered. I know I will learn, though, if only by being around some of the others who seem filled with love. Even though I feel love, I often have a difficult time expressing it. I am normally not a hugging and kissing type but when I gave Pat an embrace it seemed beautiful and natural.

Next Sunday I will be baptized and confirmed at mass. I am anxious and also excited. I see the event as the beginning of a lasting relationship, one that at times will be filled with difficulties and frustrations, but also with growth and love. That great bear of a man, Bill Harris, will be my sponsor.

Thursday, August 25, 1978

Gretchen wanted to have a party following my baptism, but I would rather have some time simply to reflect on the day in peace. Right now I feel a bit like a sacrificial lamb.

Chapter 7

A new Christian

Monday, August 28, 1978

We have a new pope, and a new Christian.

On August 26, despite the political opinions of the news media, the patriarch of Venice, Cardinal Albino Luciani, was selected to be the new pope. He named himself John Paul I, thus telling the world that he will continue the programs initiated by John and Paul. The selection occurred on the first day in conclave, surprising everyone. It was fascinating to listen to the early speculations by the news media and commentators. One would think it was a political convention. Except for a quick remark from one of the cardinals, there was no mention of the Holy Spirit providing guidance. After the selection a stir developed over "the renewal," women priests, birth control, married priests, and so on. Did anyone mention spiritual renewal?

I am the new Christian. I was baptized and confirmed by Pat yesterday. It was a beautiful experience. Baptism seemed almost a formality because I already felt baptized. Confirmation, however, was very powerful. When Pat held my head as I knelt before the altar, I was aware of an awesome power in his hands.

> All-powerful God, father of our Lord Jesus Christ, by water and the Holy Spirit you freed your son from sin and gave him new

A new Christian

life. Send your Holy Spirit upon Russ to be his helper and guide. Give him the spirit of wisdom and understanding, the spirit of knowledge and reverence. Fill him with the spirit of wonder and awe in your presence.

I was not touched by a tongue of fire but I did not expect that. Perhaps Gretchen expressed it best when she said, "There was something very special about the embrace Pat gave you at the end of confirmation. God could not have been closer than at that moment. And there was something special about seeing your arm embracing Pat, plain for all to see against the crimson of his robe." In a way it was symbolic of my touching God, as well as his touching me—a sign of an active relationship. I recall Pat's first few words to me: "He is a mystery." Now I am part of that mystery!

After mass, Pat gave me a card which read: "Today I realized I am not a thing—I am!" Inside, he had written: "Be not afraid, I go before you always. Come follow me, and I will give you rest." (Isaiah 43:2-3; Luke 6:20) Also: "Praise God for our new leader—Pope John Paul; praise God for our new Christian—Russ."

I feel a new chapter in my life beginning. I am glad that I experienced joy yesterday, and fear and anxiety the few days prior to that. I see that the road ahead is filled with both. Being a Christian is not easy. It is not standing on a corner with a perpetual look of puppy-love joy on one's face and banging a tambourine. The best work is often done in private, free from an audience. Also, being a Christian is not necessarily doing the Lord's work—he will do it anyway, in his own way and his own time. Our task is to follow where he leads us. Some will be allowed to give much in the service of others. For other men and women, "just a simple faith" is the most beautiful gift in the world.

I had no idea I was going to write this last paragraph, but I like what it says.

Yesterday I was furious at my parents for being ignorant, closed-minded idiots with whom I couldn't share my baptism and confirmation. They will surely believe I have taken leave of my senses for becoming a Catholic. Even so, I can only praise them for bringing me here. Perhaps someday I will be able to repay them. If they are not yet ready to accept my baptism, someday perhaps they will be.

Sunday, September 3, 1978

God's way is not our way. Yesterday I had to console Pat, of all people.

After I had finished rounds and taken Michelle (my daughter from California) to the beach, a bizarre chain of events occurred. Michelle was enjoying the water immensely but the surf began to rage and the red flag went up so we had to get out. Far out to sea a black wall of cloud was moving closer in a menacing way, even though the sun was still shining on the beach. Slowly, the afternoon became overcast, and the intensity of the storm began to grow.

I said a brief prayer, hoping to clear the storm, or to hold it back for a while. Suddenly a fierce wind started blowing sand everywhere, driving people from the beach to the shelter of their cars. We went home covered with sand and disappointed that we had had to leave.

About an hour later, Gretchen called from work and told us that a three-year-old child had been on the same beach when the storm arose. By a freak accident she had been speared through the chest by an umbrella pole that had been ripped into the air by the wind. The child had died.

Later, Pat called terribly upset. He knew the family and had been to see them at the hospital. He could barely get his words out. He started to cry, saying he didn't know how he could say the funeral mass. I was silent. I knew somehow he would be able to do it when the time came. I told him that I would pray for him. I have never said that to anyone before.

Sometimes things just don't make any sense. This has to be one of those events we will never understand.

Friday, September 8, 1978

I have been in a terrible frame of mind lately. For the past three days I have been under a tremendous amount of pressure. I have tension headaches daily, and I feel as if I need a vacation. Instead of taking one, though, I have been working harder, almost compulsively.

My prayers have dried up, and I have been having a terrible struggle with my application for the diaconate program. It is a burdensome affair of some fourteen pages that questions everything in one's life. I am especially bogged down with my autobiography, my reasons for wanting to become a deacon, and my strengths and weaknesses as a Catholic. At this point I only feel weak. I am also somewhat irritated that I need a psychological interview.

Monday evening, September 11, 1978

I had my psychological interview today with Father Lurton, the program psychologist. He is a somewhat distant, smirking sort of soul.

I did not appreciate the interview and felt it was somewhat peculiar that a psychologist was interviewing a psychiatrist. In an hour and fifteen minutes we discussed spirituality for perhaps two minutes. The rest of the time we talked about my life devoid of religion, my rapid move into the Church, my previous divorce, and my future plans, which consisted of very little. At one point I said I would like to become a beach bum. I must have sounded extremely unstable and sarcastic. I felt that I was being judged on where I have been, rather than on where I am. If a man converts to Christianity on his death bed, is he any less a Christian than the most devoted Catholic of fifty years?

I was also aware of some excitement on Father Lurton's part because I am a trained psychiatrist. I could see light bulbs winking on about how I could be of use. Sensing this, I tried to explain that I do very little psychiatry in my career at this point, although it is extremely useful to me as a neurologist. While my professional background may seem exciting to the program, it may be through my background of human errors—no religion, divorce, annulment—that I will have the most to offer.

Father Lurton advised me to have a spiritual director during my training, mainly because of my youth in the Church. I can see only wisdom in this suggestion. Pat has agreed to be my director.

I cannot deny that I have been moving fast. A week from Wednesday I will work with Pat for the first time as a lay eucharistic minister at the noon mass. Just the thought of it makes me nervous. I may lose the key to the tabernacle, drop the host on the floor, and spill wine all over my alb. Even so, I probably won't do any worse than that scroungy group of Apostles who often erred and stumbled following our Lord.

Wednesday, September 13, 1978

Last night with Gretchen's patient help I think I finally and very painfully confronted my main resistance to the diaconate application. It is like every commitment I have ever made. After the initial excitement I begin to balk and question what I am doing. Before I know it, I am trying to squirm out of it because it impinges upon my life. I did the same thing before Gretchen and I got married. Even though I loved her and wanted to go in that direction, I balked and felt panicky, as if I were losing myself. In my heart I knew the marriage was right, and now I know training for the diaconate is also right, but I am still afraid of taking that step.

The application is a commitment. It will involve work and personal sacrifice, but as Fausto said, "it will also involve love."

Sunday, September 17, 1978

I am finally getting into the application now. Since talking to Gretchen I feel much more at ease. Words are beginning to flow freely.

Wednesday evening, September 20, 1978

Today I functioned as a lay eucharistic minister for the first time.

I had several "walk throughs" over the past week with Pat and Brad, a second-year candidate to the diaconate, who assists at daily mass. He is a short, wiry, black engineer whom I have silently admired; he is always there, helping.

It was quiet when I arrived at the chapel. The candles had not been lit so I knew that Brad had not yet arrived. I sat alone enjoying the silence in which I could feel the presence of God.

Brad came in and started to sit in the pew in front of me. I had always sat behind him so I would know when to stand and kneel. I invited him to sit next to me. It was the first time we had ever sat together. He silently went through the rosary while I gave thanks to our Father for allowing me to be there and to share in this common meal. I asked him to continue to guide me as I joined Pat and Brad at the altar.

A new Christian

Pat came in then and helped me into my alb. The wooden cross I placed around my neck had fishes and loaves on the center of it, the sign of the lay eucharistic minister. Brad patiently guided me step by step through the mass again and Pat smiled, saying, "Just don't wash my hands with the wine."

The people stood as we walked from the sacristy to the altar. I did some fumbling (I nearly did wash Pat's hands with the wine) but generally it went well. I still do not feel comfortable crossing myself so I didn't. I did bow appropriately as that felt right.

As Pat spoke to the community about the lay eucharistic minister, I gazed out to find Gretchen in the first row. She has been working nights and sleeping during the day but insisted on coming. I must admit I was pleased to share these moments with her.

Curiously, the creed, which has continued to nag at me, filled me with a sort of comfort this time. It was as if the community of the faithful was giving me strength, and I believe I gave them something in return. Just seeing one of their own (very recent at that) going to the altar to distribute the sacred bread must mean something.

One of the high moments of the mass for me came at the kiss of peace: "I leave you peace, my peace I give you." I moved among the people, shaking their hands, young and old hands, black and white, warm, limp, full, and strong. I was smiling and reaching out with an extra effort to those who seemed reluctant; to Gretchen I gave a kiss.

As mass ended I felt warm and happy inside. "The mass is ended. Go in peace to love and serve the Lord."

Chapter 8

Learning

Sunday evening, September 24, 1978

How in the world can I ever describe my first full weekend in the diaconate program? There is so much more to it than just fourteen hours of lecture. The experience was similar to the way one teacher described the course in Church history: "This course isn't just a series of facts and dates; it's also the movement of the Spirit." Clearly, this weekend has not been merely training but spiritual growth.

The weekend began on Friday evening with forty-five men (most with their wives) gathered in a small upper room at a beach motel in Destin. The motel caters mainly to parties (and I mean parties) of fishermen preparing for a weekend of fishing after they spend most of the night getting fortified with three thousand cans of beer. Our two groups made quite a contrast. One person walks by holding a fishing pole and a can of beer, while another walks by holding a bible and a note pad. Fishers of fish and fishers of men.

We started out with two hours of lecture on Church history given by Father Nass, a bright young priest with a Ph.D. in Church history and a pleasant, dry wit. His enthusiasm about "the coming back of the deacon" immediately fired our own. He said, "You men are going to be with the people. You may do much more than many priests who are living in a rectory far from the world. God is touching you and like the Apostles you can change the world."

After Father Nass's captivating lectures about an otherwise dull subject, he and Father Fausto said mass. By the time I settled into my room that night, even though I was tired, I was so enthused I could not sleep.

Saturday morning and afternoon continued with five more hours of Church history lecture, and Father Nass beginning to lose his voice but not his enthusiasm. We had lunch together followed by a group meditation led by Father Fausto. He then sent us out to meditate on our own about some of the things he had talked about and our calling to ministry. He begged us not to go off and watch football games. (How well he knows us already!)

After a convivial dinner, preceded by a loudly-shouted "Grace!" we saw a filmstrip on the shroud of Turin, believed to be the burial shroud of Jesus. We then went over the stations of the cross. By that time I had begun to feel as if I had dropped my own cross and fallen three times, but Fausto drove us on without mercy through a holy hour and eucharistic blessing before we were excused.

Walking back to my room under a heaven lit with stars, I found myself thinking that the message is so great there should have been hundreds here instead of just forty-five. But then perhaps that is why we are here.

On Sunday we continued with mass and lectures until two in the afternoon. Father Hines, a marvelous Irish priest, gave us two very thought-provoking hours on what ministry should be, followed by two hours on how to pray. He felt that during our pursuit of ministry and holiness we should emphasize the positive rather than the negative aspects. We (especially Catholics) so often pursue a spiritual life filled with negative ideals: "I should not do this and I should not do that." We dwell on our sins and forget that we have positive features as well. If we see ourselves only as sinful and bad, he asked, how can we accept the fact that God loves us? And how can we offer love freely to others? We often try to bribe God into loving us by saying, "If I do this for the Church then God will love me." Or, "If I am good, God will be good to me." Our lives can be so conditional.

Father Hines's lecture was punctuated by many amens or alleluias from some of my classmates. At one point, Dr. Saxer, my physician friend, leaned over to me and whispered, "You're a neurologist. Can't you give them something to keep them quiet?"

When Father Hines suggested a way to pray, our whole group latched on to it. I found it curious that so many people who have been Catholics their entire lives admitted that they do not really know how to pray.

His suggestion for a scriptural prayer included five Ps: choose a Passage of scripture (about ten lines), find a Place alone, get into a relaxed Posture, become aware of the Presence of God, and read the Passage. Never rush; open yourself to listening. Make it a controlled situation by setting a ten-minute time limit. Never enter prayer thinking you have to accomplish something. Let God speak to you. Read slowly, until some thought strikes you, Father Hines told us, then stop and reflect on it. Do not go over the time limit.

In our rap session at the end of the weekend, a bit of a flap developed over ordination. It became clear that completing the program does not mean automatic ordination. If we are deemed adequate and well trained, then we may be ordained if we are acceptable to the bishop and if he has something for us to do. I am enjoying myself now and love what I'm learning from the courses. In some ways I would just as soon not be ordained; I can see it only as an opportunity for more work.

Tuesday, September 26, 1978

Last night Gretchen made a cake to celebrate Pat's fifth anniversary of ordination. Before we took it to his house she started pacing the room with a piece of paper in her hand. I finally asked her what she was doing. She said she felt overwhelmed with love for me and Pat and had written a note to bring with the cake. She was having second thoughts about the note, however, and asked me if I would read it. As I recall, it went like this:

Dear Pat,

As I reflect on your anniversary, I want to share some thoughts I have had about the cake we are giving you. It is not an ordinary cake but contains a lot of symbolism. It is round, a circle, representing the endless love of Christ. The curled edges of the frosting are like the waves of the sea, also like the love of Christ, constant, yet ever changing in our lives. The color green is the color of life, physical and spiritual, another gift from Christ. The spiritual life is such a challenge to accept. It can be quite painful and frightening at times. The cake is also very simple, the way Christ should be in our lives, not nearly so complex or so difficult to know as we often make him out to be.

Pat, all this has everything to do with you. You are Christ's instrument and I have never known such a fine one. Your life is truly spiritual. You represent Christ in a way I have never known, and in a way Russ is so fortunate to know. You have also shown us the true beauty and simplicity of Christ, in spite of some of his complexity. For all of these things we thank you and need you. Our very best wishes and our love to you,

Gretchen and Russ

What beauty. If all these feelings can be conveyed with a simple cake, think of what can be present in the bread and wine, "the treasure that Jesus left for all of us," as Pat described it this past Sunday.

I tried to convince Gretchen that if I cut a piece of cake for myself before we brought it to Pat it would also symbolize our humanness but she wouldn't allow that.

Friday, September 29, 1978

Pope John Paul I died last night of an apparent heart attack after only thirty-four days as pope. It took everyone by surprise.

His death stirs our emotions and raises many questions. I suppose everyone has a different theory as to its meaning. I do not see it as a bad omen; a human tragedy, yes; a divine tragedy, of course not. He was like a breath of fresh air with his wonderful humanness and his warm smile, and that has been gift enough for me. I am sure that Jesus often gave nothing more, and yet touched the hearts of many.

I am sorry to see our new pope pass so soon. In a way I loved him without even knowing him. I recall my baptism when Pat said, "We have a new pope and a new Christian." John Paul and I were linked briefly and now he is gone, but I must go on. I hope that I, too, will bring a breath of fresh air, humanness, and a warm smile to the Church.

Sunday afternoon, October 1, 1978

I served as a lay eucharistic minister today for the first time at a Sunday mass. The large number of people made it difficult for me to relax. As Pat and I walked up the aisle my knees trembled. During communion I kept hitting people on the upper lip with the host and was caught totally by surprise when one fellow came up with his hands held out and his mouth open at the same time. I didn't know where to put the host until he lunged at it with his mouth, nearly getting one of my fingers. When we walked down the aisle at the end of mass I was almost expecting people to hurl banana peels and eggs at me.

Monday, October 2, 1978

I just tried to do a ten-minute scriptural prayer. I set out to pick something in the Gospels but started reading Jeremiah, my old friend. The words in chapter thirty, "Write all the words I have spoken to you in a book," set me into a great stir. I feel as if they were meant for me.

I planned to re-read the passage and meditate on it but first I decided to sit silently and clear my mind. I was rather startled to discover that I was expecting something from my prayer. I tried to abandon my expectations and open myself to the Father. It wasn't easy. My mind was hanging on its hinges, painfully slow to open. As the door finally began to swing ajar, just a crack, my mind was filled with a startling thought: "You shall have a son, John Paul." Nothing more.

I do not understand and feel afraid. Are Gretchen and I to have a son? Perhaps I am fabricating lines in my own mind. And yet they must be God's; they certainly don't feel like mine even though I write them. I wonder, Lord, what are you doing?

Thursday, October 5, 1978

Pope John Paul I was buried in the grotto of St. Peter's Basilica yesterday afternoon. As Cardinal Carlo Confalonieri, Dean of the College of Cardinals, looked down on a sea of umbrellas in the rain, he said, "He passed as a meteor which unexpectedly lights up the heavens and then disappears, leaving us amazed and astonished." Then he continued, "It is not the length which characterizes a life in a pontificate but rather the spirit that fills it."

Sunday evening, October 8, 1978

I was a lay eucharistic minister today for Father Dawson. What a disaster! The only thing I did right was get his newspaper out of the car so he could read the baseball scores. (He started mass with a prayer that the Dodgers beat the Yankees in the World Series. Amen from me on that one.)

During mass I didn't know what Father Dawson was going to do from one moment to the next. When we walked in to stand before the altar, he turned to me and whispered, "Let's sit down." I sat on the end seat leaving an empty chair in the middle for him. He sat on the chair at the other end. Before I knew it he was standing again. I looked around and saw that I was the only one in the whole church still seated. I tried to rise gently to my feet so no one would notice but everyone did; the entire choir was snickering.

My only task at the altar was to put the tops back on the cruets of wine and water. I tried to wash Father's hands but he took the cruet from my hand and did it himself. At communion my hands shook again. I hit the commanding officer of the naval air station on the upper lip with the host and he glared at me as if I were a clumsy frog. When I approached the choir with communion they stared at me blankly. I finally realized that Father Dawson had already given them communion. The whole experience was absolutely miserable.

Tuesday, October 10, 1978

Last night Pat started his new series of bible classes. I cannot believe it was only eight months ago that I attended the same class. What an amazing year it has been. My growth has been unbelievable—last year I was a passive, skeptical observer, and this year I am an active, skeptical believer. In less than a year I have come to help distribute the sacred bread at the table of God. I still do not understand, but I am here.

Pat's teaching nicely complemented our training in the diaconate. He began by discussing how the Bible was written in faith and can only be understood in faith. Scripture is our experience of listening to God.

Listening. How often have I listened to God, or just been aware of his presence for even five minutes? The same old question. In my growth I would love to say I do this frequently, but I don't. I am usually doing the talking.

A literal interpretation of the Bible is the most obvious one, Pat explained. But we must be aware that there is a deeper meaning, for to look deeper is to grow. We can never learn too much about the Bible.

Tuesday evening, October 10, 1978

I am struggling again. I find it very difficult to be a doctor, a writer, and a candidate to the diaconate while trying to be a husband and still find some free time. I have always loved to be a student and work hard, yet now when I am assigned readings for the diaconate training, I balk and struggle. Reading has become a chore. I don't know when to fit it in. At times I wish I didn't have to go to work—I have found so many other things I prefer to do. Last night for a few minutes I considered dropping out of the program. I, of all people, have every reason to withdraw; no one would be surprised. The pressure would subside and I would be free again.

Since I was brought to this by the Lord, I went to pray and discuss it with him. If he wants me here, he can help me. He didn't answer. Not a word. He makes me angry. He sets the hook in me when he chooses, but when I start struggling and ask for help, he says nothing.

Wednesday, October 11, 1978

Take, bless, break, and share. Pat said some interesting things in his homily today about these four words: they are always an important part of the mass. We take bread, bless it, break it, and share it, but at the same time we take our own lives, bless ourselves, break our lives into many different areas, and share our joys and sufferings.

After mass, Pat gave me a beautiful medal of Mary, the Blessed Mother. It was inscribed on the back: "Blessed lady, pray that I continue to strive to follow your son in the spirit life." It was dated August 27, 1978, the date of my baptism and confirmation. As I write these words I feel tears in my eyes, tears of love for Pat and all that he has given me. I am also hoping to take my life, bless it, break it among others, and share it. At this moment I am wearing the medal as a reminder to pray for a young man I admitted to the hospital this afternoon.

Terry Wilson was referred to me by an eye doctor because of the sudden onset of double vision a few days ago. He is a twenty-eight-year-old, friendly but somewhat frightened flight instructor with light sandy hair and a slight stutter. He was accompanied by his radiant young wife who was cradling a three-week-old baby in her arms. I am sure there is something terribly wrong with him.

Besides the double vision he has been having spells of dizziness, morning headaches, and vomiting. During my examination I noted papilledema, a sign of increased intracranial pressure. My training and my senses say he has a brain tumor. I did an EEG and found some intermittent frontal slow wave activity, often the sign of a deep midline mass or a frontal tumor. As I await the results of his CT brain scan, I am hoping and praying that he does not have a tumor. With this medal around my neck, I pray that I can help this man and his family. Father, more so than in mine, he is in your hands now. Please help him.

Thursday, October 12, 1978

Terry Wilson has a brain tumor. His CT scan revealed a large tumor in the right frontal lobe, creating a great deal of edema and shift of the midline. I have been working all day trying to find out how to airevacuate him to Bethesda for neurosurgery. Things look bleak.

I told Terry and his wife the grim news. Their faces fell and his wife mumbled something like, "I knew it." They cried and sat clinging to each other for a few minutes. I tried to pray during that silence but the experience took the wind out of my sails.

I have the strangest inner sensation that Terry Wilson and I are going to be linked together somehow—that we are just beginning some sort of relationship. I don't understand it.

Monday afternoon, October 16, 1978

Because of my delay in getting Terry transferred to Bethesda, Gretchen and I had to race to get down to Destin for the diaconate training weekend. We made it with fifteen minutes to spare. Now I can hardly believe it is all over and I am back at the hospital again.

I had some trouble this time; it developed Saturday morning. Sessions begin with morning prayer which has generally been a rosary. As I came into the room Fausto and I greeted each other with a hug. Then he asked me (as always) how I was doing. I mumbled, "Fine," and then before I knew it I had decided to tell him how I really felt. I told him I didn't like the rosary. For me it was the longest part of the entire weekend. He raised his eyebrows and said that I should skip it. So we talked outside the room while everyone else said the rosary. The whole time I could hear the Hail Marys echoing through the wall.

It was a good talk. I told him that I felt awkward saying the rosary although I could see the value of it for others. He explained something about its origin, how it was used in the Middle Ages to mark the passage of time for meditation and prayer, and how when the mass used to be mysterious, with the priest facing the altar and murmuring in Latin, it was something tangible for the faithful to hold on to. But he said that if I remained uncomfortable with it, I should make a private meditation or use scripture for my morning prayer. I like that idea but at the same time I feel a little guilty because the rosary is a community activity, and I feel I should be present. On the other hand if I only become irritated and angry sitting with the group, it would be better to do what Fausto suggested. He is our director, so why not?

Pat came down Saturday morning and sat in on Father Reardon's lecture on the travels of Paul. Once again the lectures were outstanding but by four o'clock in the afternoon I felt as if a steam roller had run over my head. The pace can be intense.

After a brief private meditation, we had two hours of pastoral counseling, four more hours of lecture on scripture (essentially on

Acts and the writings of Paul), four more hours on Church history and liturgy, and finally a funny presentation by Father Fausto on moral theology, Italian style, which was right on target.

I would love to write more about the weekend because so much happened, but today has been extremely busy and I'm tired. I have been running all over the hospital seeing consults for twitching arms, dementia, seizures, and other neurologic disorders. An important aspect of being a deacon is remaining with the people, and today people have occupied most of my time. If I have done all I can for these people who are sick, then I feel I have done all I can both as a doctor and as a Christian.

Later, Monday afternoon, October 16, 1978

Pat just called. We have a new pope. I can't pronounce his name but he is a fifty-eight-year-old cardinal from Poland, the first non-Italian pope to be elected in 450 years. He has chosen the name John Paul II. It's beautiful to see the unity in our faith. My meditation of a few nights ago strikes me as even more curious now: "You shall have a son, John Paul."

Tuesday, October 17, 1978

After the weekend of powerful teaching I still wanted to attend Pat's bible session last night. I'm glad I did because Pat said some important things.

The Bible is written for each of us, Pat explained, and God can touch our lives through this book. At times we get caught up in the "backward trend," that is, "Back when God was God and did this and that...." But he is with us now, exactly as he was "back then." He communicates in the same way, through creation, conscience, and scripture. When Abraham was called it was not by a voice—the communication was by the Spirit. I have recorded some of my experiences in this book. I have never "heard" words, but have "felt" them. I am acting as an instrument for someone else. Unfortunately, I have to take this experience and write it down on paper; I must take something intangible and try to make it tangible so others can understand. And by that very process something is lost.

Just as God spoke to men and women of faith "back then," he is speaking to us now if we only listen. God loves each of us and his love is so unconditional it is nearly beyond comprehension. We find it difficult to believe that there are no strings attached. I still struggle with that; I still think I have to do something for his love. And I still doubt him at times and question him frequently. He doesn't seem to mind.

Tuesday, October 24, 1978

The reality of the hospital keeps life in perspective for me. Almost every time I get wrapped up in my own trivial disasters, some real disaster occurs.

Yesterday, Mrs. Marco, a fifty-five-year-old short and slightly plump woman, got out of bed to prepare her husband's coffee as she has been doing for the past thirty years. Suddenly she had a severe, frighteningly painful headache and collapsed to the floor. When she arrived at the emergency room she was unresponsive and the family was in shock. They kept repeating, "We were just talking to her."

As the day went on it became apparent that she was not going to survive. Her respirations became irregular and her pupils became fixed and dilated. Ice-water calorics did not make her eyes deviate from the midline. I did a spinal tap and grossly bloody spinal fluid rose to the top of the manometer and flowed over. She had a subarachnoid hemorrhage, probably the result of a burst aneurysm. Talking to the family was a nightmare as I tried to explain that even though her heart was still beating, her brain was irreparably damaged. We mutually decided not to use a respirator.

Unexpectedly, her husband came to see her at the very moment her heart was beginning to slow down. The nurses and I were standing behind the curtain feeling helpless and alone in our own misery when he came through the opening. He looked down at his wife, put his hands to his face, and started to choke and sob. She looked terrible; her skin had turned a blotchy blue. She was not breathing at all, and the cardiac monitor was making only a rare beep every few seconds. The nurse next to me had just removed a set of wedding rings from her swollen fingers (circles without beginning, without end). She held them tightly in her hand, wisely feeling that to hand them to the husband at that moment was not appropriate. The hospital chaplain entered at the same time and tried to comfort Mr. Marco, whose face had become pale and drawn. Finally the chaplain gently led him away.

As the cardiac monitor converted to a straight line I continued to look down at Mrs. Marco, realizing how fragile our lives are. This woman was alive just hours ago doing what she has done every morning for years, and now her life was over.

As all became quiet behind the curtain I imagined myself looking down at Gretchen. Losing her is beyond my comprehension. The thought continued to nag at the corners of my mind most of last night at home. After Gretchen left for her night shift I spent a few minutes on my knees letting the same thoughts flow over me. I could not comprehend everlasting life; I could see only the end of life.

I remembered my first encounter with God, when one of my patients was dying, and I was suddenly filled with a sense of peace— peace and everlasting life. Thoughts and feelings swirled around me. There is peace, yet I cannot explain it, and at the moment I do not feel it either.

Wednesday, October 25, 1978

During noon mass today my thoughts about Mrs. Marco and the sudden changes in life continued. I wondered if Terry Wilson was having brain surgery at this very moment or whether he was even still alive.

When I tipped the cup of wine to drink, I saw myself reflected back from the bottom of the cup. "Take this, all of you and drink from it: this is the cup of my blood, the blood of the new and everlasting covenant. It will be shed for you. Do this in memory of me." I saw my eyes staring back from the depths of the mystery of the cup. The reflection startled me. I have become part of this mystery. We are all part of it, a mystery we cannot fully comprehend, in life or in death. I pray for Mr. Marco and hope that somehow in time he can understand. I also pray for Terry Wilson and his family, and even for myself, because I don't know where I am going.

Saturday, October 28, 1978

I have been nailed to the cross. I just called two of my closest friends who live in Maryland. I thought they would be interested to know that this heathen soul has become a Catholic convert. Now I wonder if it was a mistake.

Ken was aghast and thought I had taken leave of my senses. After he had recovered from his shock, he said, with just a hint of genuine interest, that he would like to talk with me about it sometime. I felt that it might be to try to convert me back.

The other friend and his wife responded at first with chuckles and then concern that Gretchen had somehow twisted my arm to get me to enter the Church. That made me angry and I told them that Gretchen did not have anything to do with my conversion and that I was enjoying myself immensely. Perhaps because they are fallen-away Catholics they became defensive, speaking of the rigidity of the new pope and how the Church is still in the dark ages. I responded with my own defensiveness, saying I didn't think they really knew what the Church is all about. "What do you mean? We have been Catholics all our lives," they responded. "You have just been dazzled."

There wasn't much sense in continuing. I had flashbacks of our many talks over the past few years, our quiet evenings together. This occasion was the first time we had ever disagreed strongly. I don't understand. I thought my news would bring us closer together. Instead it seems it could easily drive us apart.

I am sure that when the time comes to tell my parents about my conversion I will have to stand by to resuscitate them. I know they will blame Gretchen.

"I have come with the sword."

Tuesday, October 31, 1978

"Let us pause for a moment and reflect on how we have been aware of God in our lives in the past week." Pat often opens the penitential rite in this way, but then before I am able even to begin reflecting he starts talking again. Yesterday after mass I decided to tell him about it. We walked back to his office, bundling our khaki windbreakers around us to keep out the early chill of winter. His colorful notes and reminders were all over the office as usual.

I told him how I felt when he begins the penitential rite. Too many times I cannot remember spending any time with God in the past week and I grumbled that we should have a few more seconds or even a minute to reflect seriously on this omission. I thought Pat might be offended but he agreed and plans to expand that time. He is so incredibly open. I hope someday I can be as open to change or constructive suggestions as he is.

Pat's bible classes continue to be fascinating. He is using more filmstrips and is really beginning to express his feelings about scripture. This past week he spoke of Moses, and how we must all "wander in the desert" at times, unsure of what we are doing. It is often in that lonely desert that we become aware of God in our lives. He again emphasized how he felt that Moses communicated with God inwardly, not with words. I thought it was interesting that Moses used so many excuses to avoid going back to Egypt at God's command. "I stutter. Why me? What will people think?" It all sounds so familiar.

Tonight is Pat's birthday and Gretchen and I are going to his house for dinner. I am going to show some slides I have collected on the shroud of Turin and we are going to give him a small picture of a glass of wine and a loaf of bread. Below it are the words: "To sacrifice something is to make it holy, by giving it away for love." The words aren't terribly clear to my slow mind, but I like them. Pat's life seems to revolve around the bread and wine and I know he will appreciate the gift.

Thursday, November 9, 1978

I haven't written in a long time. I have been busy preparing a manuscript on "The Psychiatric Aspects of Headache" for a symposium being presented in Las Vegas in early December. Writing it has given me a headache. Fortunately I am finished now.

I talked to my friend Dennis, who did the neurosurgery on Terry Wilson, last week. He found an angry-appearing tumor spread throughout most of the frontal lobe. He could not get it all and he is currently treating Terry with radiation. The outlook is bleak. From the latest statistics, fifty percent of patients treated with both surgery and radiation die within nine months, and ninety-five percent within eighteen months. I pray that he may be in the last five percent.

Monday, November 13, 1978

The diaconate training weekend was long and hard. The teaching was again superb but I struggled with my own feelings through much of it.

Friday night Father Lurton appeared out of his psychological closet to work with us for two hours on pastoral counseling, using mainly transactional analysis techniques (parent-adult-child interactions on an I'm ok, you're ok level). When we divided into groups I volunteered to help out as a supervisor because of my background as a psychiatrist. That offer set the tone for the weekend. It seemed that every five minutes some troubled soul appeared at my door asking for help with an emotional problem. After the evening mass, Fausto invited me to his room where we went over some problems he is having with a person he is counseling.

Gretchen was sound asleep when I got in at eleven. She would have to leave in the morning because of work. Too wound up to sleep, I stared at a late movie, watching a vampire suck the life out of his victims, wondering why psychiatry had to come up again at this point in my life.

The night passed fitfully and I started out Saturday morning feeling worn out, unrevived even by two cups of coffee. Father Dawson went over the epistles of Paul for four hours. He showed how each one revealed a bit more evolution in style, as if Paul were slowly crystallizing his thinking as he wrote. Then he considered the words Paul used, what he meant by *grace, peace*, and *apostle*. Once again the holy scriptures came alive for me.

The next four hours were on Church history by Father Nass, our "little monk," as we have affectionately started calling him. He is a beautiful human being. We had a brief talk at lunchtime and one thing he said encouraged me. He told a story about a woman who was suicidal and unable to get in touch with him because he was removed from the world in the dusty stacks of a library, studying history. When she finally reached him she was furious at him for not being available, and he wondered what his efforts in history would ever come to. But now his involvement with us has become a highlight of his life, something he never expected.

I didn't really want to be the local shrink for the group this weekend. In some ways I find my psychiatric training burdensome, but maybe God wanted me to use my talent this weekend for the good of others.

Learning

Saturday at about 3:30 p.m. we had a half-hour meditation time and I desperately wanted to get away for a while and watch a football game. (There was no way I could have meditated at that point.) As I rushed out the door, a big fellow with a a balding head and a sad face blocked my way and asked quietly, "Did Fausto speak to you about me?" Well, Fausto hadn't. The man wanted to talk about his wife who was having back pain and about some difficulties of his own. There went the half-hour. I barely had time to run to the bathroom and back to class. By dinner I wanted to wear a sign around my neck saying, "The psychiatrist is out."

Another restless night. Sunday we had moral theology, liturgy, and mass. My pen was moving slower and slower and my mind finally ground to a halt about 11:30 a.m. when we had a break. One of the fellows asked for some help to dump the trash and I left the room so I wouldn't have to do it. My good will and my strength were both exhausted. A few minutes later I heard the fellow grumbling to Fausto that nobody would help with the trash. The next thing I knew I was dragging out a huge plastic bag. Later, during a group discussion on what we should be doing as deacons, the word "service" kept recurring. I finally told the group that I didn't know if I could take it. Instant silence. I went on to say there were times I felt I just couldn't give any more and if asked, I would look around hoping someone else would volunteer. Then I found myself saying that it was like my experience of being a doctor. In the middle of the night when the phone rings I often say, "Damn!" But then I pick up the receiver. With that comment I realized that I do give service; I just don't always give it with a smile.

As we concluded our weekend, Fausto said, "One cannot give what one does not have. If we do not have an ongoing relationship with God how can we possibly help others with theirs?" I felt like the bottom of a rock. My prayer life lately has been terrible. The relationship that started out with so much fervor seems to have become stagnant. I left feeling that I had to get back to my prayer life.

Last night I was too worn out to attend Pat's bible class so I snuggled into bed with Gretchen and while she went to sleep, I watched a football game. When the game ended I decided I should pray. I felt more tuned in and open than I had in a month.

The prayer was somewhat strange. "Nineveh" continued to come into my mind. I couldn't connect the word with anything. I looked it up in my bible dictionary: it was a city that had been flattened somewhere along the line. I looked in vain for something encouraging in the text. Finally I threw in the towel and told God, "All right, if you want to flatten me and walk on me—go ahead." This morning I saw the prayer in a new light. It is the world that has grown spiritually flat, flat as the dead city of Nineveh.

In a way I felt God was sad. Despite his giving us his son and inspiring the Bible, we continue to be distant and increasingly oriented to our physical lives. We go to church on Sunday and say a token prayer, then we go back to our houses and do not make room for God in our lives. In our neighborhood we are surrounded by Catholics who "don't go to church anymore," but nevertheless have a party for their infant's baptism. I have been working at church, distributing the holy eucharist, reading, but not praying. During my first prayer in a long time, though, he was there.

Thursday, November 16, 1978

I have been selected for commander. I can't believe it! My parents are coming to live in Pensacola. I can't believe that either.

Pat and I had an excellent session yesterday after mass. After I told him all about my "psychiatric" weekend, he pointed out that my first responsibility should be as a student in the diaconate program, and not as a psychiatrist. I can see this clearly now, and I really was aware of it during the weekend, but the schedule was so hectic there that I lost my perspective. I'm going to talk to Fausto. I should be present as a student, not as the class shrink.

I'm trying again to make a concentrated effort at daily prayer. It seems like one of the easiest things to put aside and the most difficult to do regularly.

Monday, November 20, 1978

Yesterday, browsing in a bookstore, I was nearly overwhelmed by the number of religious and spiritual books I saw. As I glanced at title after title I found myself asking, what I am writing this book for? What can I possibly say that hasn't already been said? I have never written a book; nobody knows who I am. Who will care about all this rambling from such an ordinary person?

As I continued to search the shelves I became uneasy with all of the pure, unadulterated joy presented in many of the books. I had always thought that Christians were supposed to be joyful, loving, and peaceful at all times, and if they weren't then something was wrong. However, during my brief journey in the Church, and in my work in neurology and psychiatry, I cannot say I have seen anyone in constant joy, unless he or she was manic and needed medication. I do see a great number of people searching for constant happiness, but this search for perfection more often than not leads to our undoing. If we were meant to be on cloud nine all the time we would have been issued wings and harps. We humans do not like pain and suffering, so we forget (or ignore) the meaning of death and the cross.

Meanwhile, as I read Paul's writings I am struck by the difficulties he had, his searchings and suffering. It seems that even in suffering and only in struggling do we actually learn, and by learning, begin to experience peace.

Chapter 9

Prayer

Tuesday, November 21, 1978

I have finally managed to get back to "almost" daily prayer.

For the past two or three nights though, I haven't felt tuned in. If anything, I have been getting the impression that I am wandering away from God, or have the potential to wander.

I used to enjoy the sudden scriptural inspirations that would come to me but lately they don't come, or if they do I am not sure I believe them. I am beginning to think that my own mind is quoting passages and I am not comfortable believing my own mind. Last night I even wondered if I were a "false prophet" of sorts. Perhaps we *are* supposed to be filled with joy all the time. I just don't know.

If my writing is in error I pray that the Lord will at least use it as an example of what he does not want us to be. If I illustrate how *not* to wander, then I guess I have done something.

And if the Lord wants to have a world of "puppy love" and I interfere with his plans, I can only apologize for my own humanness and failure to see the truth.

Prayer

Wednesday, November 22, 1978

Today I found a little prayer by Thomas Merton on a prayer card. It is called "Thoughts in Solitude," and it seems to speak to me:

> I have no idea where I am going. I do not see the road ahead of me. I cannot know for certain where it will end. Nor do I really know myself, and the fact that I think I am following your will does not mean that I am actually doing so.
>
> But I believe that the desire to please you does in fact please you and I hope I have that desire in all that I am doing. I hope that I will never do anything apart from that desire and I know that if I do this, you will lead me by the right road, though I may know nothing about it.
>
> Therefore, I will trust you always, though I may seem to be lost in the shadow of death. I will not fear, for you are ever with me, and you will never leave me to face my dangers alone.

Friday evening, November 24, 1978

God has allowed me a brief period in his presence.

In my evening prayer tonight I became aware of the difficulty I have been experiencing all week, beginning with "Nineveh," and followed by feelings of wandering from God and sadness. Although I have been tuned in to something, I realize now that it has not been something for me. While it has been good to be aware of my own wandering, what I have been sensing has been a divine mourning over another who wandered away.

Disaster occurred in Jonestown, Guyana, as the Reverend Jim Jones wandered from the path and lured a whole flock into mass suicide. Nearly eight hundred people—who in their fervor to become close to God missed him in the worst sort of way—died. Just as the inhabitants of Nineveh perished but left the name of the city as a reminder to us, so did those at Jonestown. And from this event, a few will return to our true shepherd.

Saturday evening, November 25, 1978

I am asking to be closer to God.

Tonight I began my prayer with an Our Father and gave thanks for my life. I thought of Jesus and Mary and what they have given us. I prayed for guidance in my upcoming lecture on the medical apsects of the shroud of Turin.

I then asked for God's help in healing Terry Wilson, in ridding him of his tumor. I most likely will not see him again but I suddenly wanted to pray for his life. I myself do not wish to have healing powers. I am afraid of misusing this type of grace, or letting it go to my head. I prefer to ask for an intercession. I realized that if Terry were to be healed, though, I would want to take some of the credit. I felt ashamed and asked God to forgive me. I prayed to know God better.

Sunday, November 26, 1978

Our minds simply cannot grasp a time or place that is unending. We look at the heavens and wonder how far away they are. Our lives, meanwhile, are a series of continuous wanderings in time, moving to the rhythm of the rising and setting of the sun and our own daily heart beat.

Tonight in my prayer I was allowed to journey for a few moments into a place of timeless peace. There was no sun, yet there was light in the darkness. It was like a deep blue sky that precedes and reveals an early sunrise. This place was easy to grasp, yet totally incomprehensible. It was life at the moment of death. I felt no fear. At the same time I had an almost detached urge to cling to my body. I did not want to give up the loves that I have on earth, but then, I do not have to give them up because they are part of the kingdom. In eternity there is no separation from love. Eternity is love.

Wednesday, November 29, 1978

Yesterday Pat and I met for our weekly spiritual direction session. I let him read the last two pages about my prayer. I felt awkward and unsure of what I had written; I was afraid I might have been on a "head trip." He explained that spiritual life *is* a sort of head trip. We humans are always trying to separate our physical life from our spiritual life, instead of realizing that they are one and the same. We are so aware of the physical aspects of our lives that when we have a deep meditation or a spiritual experience we tend to feel awkward and uncomfortable about it.

As we discussed this further I became aware of the importance of a daily prayer life. I have tended in the past to be extremely sporadic about prayer. On a daily basis it becomes a continuum, and the relationship becomes one that is constantly growing. There may be individual days of silence or confusion but in time the experiences begin to come together and transform one's entire life. A person doesn't become a concert pianist in one lesson, but only over time, which involves frustrating practice, errors, discipline, and effort. Prayer is the same.

The biggest stumbling block in prayer is silence, especially for Americans. We don't know how to handle it. Our lives are so filled with noise and clutter that we must have music, TV, or pinball machines to fill up any emptiness. When we are suddenly confronted with a period of silence we come face to face with ourselves, an experience that is both terrifying and anxiety-provoking. Yet this blessed "silence" is where we find God in our soul.

Tuesday, December 5, 1978

We had a meeting last night for all the diaconate candidates in Pensacola. Father Fausto took me aside and told me that the two priests I had asked to write letters of recommendation for my application to the diaconate program recommended that I not become a deacon. They thought I was "too new, and chasing a rainbow." Fausto slapped me on the back and told me not to worry about it; we must be open to the Spirit, who often comes when we least expect it. He has decided to keep me and thinks the bishop will too. It seems that following the Spirit is the only thing I can do at this point.

Friday, December 8, 1978

Pat has orders to go to Cuba in May or June. I cannot think about this now. What will I do without him?

Monday, December 11, 1978

Another whirlwind training weekend.

Friday afternoon I had to race like mad to get there on time. If ever I envied Paul and all his journeys, I don't anymore. I arrived just in time to stumble into my room, change clothes, tuck away my lettuce and salad makings (for the weekend lunch) and jog to the conference room. There were warm hugs and embraces of greeting before the silk-tongued Father Lurton began his two-hour lecture on pastoral counseling.

We divided into groups and I assisted again as an advisor. For some reason I was overly critical of the poor souls who were doing their best in a thirty-minute time frame to learn to listen to the problems of others. Trying too hard to be helpful, I found myself interrupting inappropriately, shooting people down, and generally making a perfect ass of myself.

We concluded Friday night with the Mass of the Immaculate Conception. I had trouble with the words to the hymns again so I kept my head down, listened to the music, and meditated about Mary. I had some difficulty understanding the concepts of sin and immaculate conception. I could remember Pat once said that Mary was rarely mentioned in the Bible, but when she was, she was described simply as, "a believer." So in her memory, I chose to believe in her and accept her immaculate conception. Usually I make a great stir about believing in anything new, but with Mary I felt at peace. I was touched by the fact that she didn't passively accept her role; she was confused and afraid at first too, so why should I worry?

Saturday passed quickly with one lecture after another. Father Reardon chain-smoked his way through three hours of scripture, dealing with the resurrection according to Paul. Paul began with the "fact" that Jesus is "risen." He emphasized that knowing the risen Jesus (Christ) is more important than knowing the earthly Jesus (perhaps echoing Paul's own conversion experience). In the latter part of 1 Corinthians he says, "What is sown is raised; perishable becomes imperishable; contemptible becomes glorious; weak becomes powerful; the soul-body (the natural thing that all men have) becomes spirit-body;" through belief and baptism we come to share in the spiritual. There is a continuity between our lives and the spiritual life; we become spiritual by a mysterious transformation, like caterpillars turning into butterflies.

Mass was celebrated by Bishop Gracida. It was the first time I had ever seen a bishop and I was deeply moved by his presence. He has majestic black hair and his face is youthful but filled with wisdom. After mass, he joined us in one of the cottages for lunch, where we all shivered together over steaming bowls of soup. The temperature had dropped to thirty degrees (not typical for Florida) and the wind was howling over the bay and right under the door.

After lunch, we picked up our chairs and walked back through the cold afternoon air to listen to the last of Father Nass's lectures on Church history. When he finished his words of wisdom on the history of the papacy up to Vatican II, the entire class rose in unison and gave him a standing ovation. His eyes filled with tears and for the first time in the lecture series he was speechless. We are really going to miss him. He then gave us something to remember him by—a take-home examination on Church history. Where I will find the time for this I have no idea.

After our "lousy rap session," as Fausto put it (because nobody wanted to say anything), we adjourned for a social hour. Back in my room a little later, I became acutely aware of how much I was missing Gretchen. Between our two schedules the past week we have hardly seen each other.

Sunday began with two hours on music in the liturgy. Then Fausto delivered a two-hour dissertation on moral theology, covering that hornet's nest of controversy, *Humanae Vitae*.

We concluded our weekend with mass, during which Fausto spoke to the children of the candidates about what Christmas means. One cute little nine-year-old boy told Fausto that he was sure that his parents would give him some presents for Christmas because they loved him. Fausto then asked, "What would you do if they were rotten and didn't love you?" I sat there stunned, wondering what I would answer to that question if he were to ask me. The little boy adjusted his glasses, scratched his head, looked at Fausto and replied, "If they were rotten, I would share some of my love with them so they would have some too." Fausto picked him up, held him high, and kissed him on the top of the head. Then he hugged him and said, "From the mouths of babes...."

Sunday, December 17, 1978
Altoona, Pennsylvania

It is only twenty-six degrees outside and the overcast sky is threatening to bring more snow. We arrived here almost a week ago, leaving the relative warmth of Pensacola for the wintry climate of Pennsylvania. From Pittsburgh we drove with Gretchen's sister over the mountains to Altoona. As we crept over the mountain road through the light snow flurry, we chattered away, trying to fill in the gaps of information that separation causes.

We arrived at Gretchen's house in the middle of a "retirement-Christmas party" for Uncle Joe, who was retiring from his job at the bakery. Behind Uncle Joe's air of jocularity and tears of joy were many tears of sadness. He is running on one coronary artery and has frequent chest pains that are beyond the treatment capabilities of his doctors. He is living from moment to moment, drinking and smoking with great gusto, and waiting.

Despite the holiday symbols, the pervading atmosphere of sadness also surrounds Gretchen's mother. Even though there are brilliant lights shining on the Christmas tree, presents, cookies, and quiet Christmas carols, everyone knows her life flame is beginning to flicker. Her face is drawn and sallow and her gentle frame has been ravaged and thinned by cancer and the devasting treatments. Most of the time she is confused and just lies on the couch; at the dinner table she picks at her food, sometimes forgetting to raise the fork to her mouth. Her husband helps her through the day in the most tender and loving manner, but at night he sits alone in front of the television, numbing his aching heart with whiskey until early morning.

Today at mass I was suddenly struck with the thought of Gretchen's mother at home, unable to come to church because of her illness. I wondered if perhaps I could take her communion.

After mass, I approached the young parish priest and asked him if I could take communion to her. He smiled and said, "That's a lovely idea and I would give you permission in an instant." Moving closer and touching my arm, he added, "I want you to know I love the lay ministry movement that is sweeping the country. Unfortunately it stopped when it arrived at the edge of Altoona. You see, our pastor doesn't believe in it and I'm afraid you will have to ask him." Gretchen and I looked at each other and our shoulders sagged.

Father O'Brien is an older Irish priest, known equally for his conservative rigidity and his forgetfulness (highlighted last Christmas by his greeting the people at midnight mass with a rousing, "Happy Easter!") We found him hobbling around in the back of the church, his legs being a source of chronic difficulty for him because of poor circulation. I introduced myself and he ignored me, giving his attention instead to Gretchen. He lighted a cigarette and then directed his steely gaze at me, peering over the top of his bifocals as if I were an obstacle in his way. I forced out my question about communion for Gretchen's mother. His facial expression did not change as he rocked back and forth on his heels. He gave a polite little cough and attempted to dismiss the matter by saying that he had just spoken with her on the phone and she would be coming to mass. We explained that she wasn't really able to travel. He started rocking again and exhaled a long stream of smoke. Suddenly, he stared me right in the eye and said that he would be happy to come over later in the day to hear her confession; then I could take her communion on Christmas. Gretchen and I walked away thinking he must have been nipped by the Christmas spirit.

Sunday, Christmas Eve, 1978

Snow was falling, quietly blanketing the cars and streets, when the family set out to walk the two blocks to church to attend midnight mass. It was my first time at a midnight service, and will probably be my last.

As both priests began the eucharistic prayer, a pretty girl with long hair suddenly slumped over the railing right in front of us. For a few seconds she stayed like that, then suddenly she pitched back and stiffened. I stood and reached for her, trying to lay her down on the bench. Her family was getting hysterical and just as eagerly tried to prop her up. I almost shouted at them that I was a doctor and she needed to lie down. Gretchen at my side was telling them (a bit more kindly) the same thing. The scuffling and confusion intensified as I tried to untangle the girl's feet from the kneeler. In the background I was aware of the hush in the church as every eye was riveted on the growing chaos in the pew, and from the altar the words droned on: "On the night he was betrayed, he took bread and gave you thanks...." Finally, Gretchen and I got the girl flat and the family quiet. As soon as the girl's head was lowered, her eyelids fluttered open and she awoke from her faint, startled and feeling ill. Members of her family helped her from the church.

As the service continued, the pastor started swinging the censer of incense back and forth over the altar and clanged it into the chalice, knocking the cardboard pall from it and nearly toppling the cup.

During the last few minutes of the mass I reflected that as we were praising the birth of Jesus, it seemed as if all should be peaceful. But as long as the human element is present I doubt if we will ever have that ultimate peace.

Monday, Christmas, 1978

After the presents were opened Christmas morning I started up the icy snow-covered street to get the eucharist from Father O'Brien. The snow was whipped into my face by a chill wind that howled through the quiet streets. Father O'Brien greeted me at the rectory and told me that he had everything ready for me. Unfortunately, he had forgotten where he put the pyx. As he rummaged through cupboards and drawers, I sighed inwardly and sat listening to the wind whistling against the church windows. Finally he found the small carrying case and went stumping off to the altar on his old man's legs to get the host.

As I started back to the house, the wind died down and I reflected, with some degree of amazement, on what I was doing. Just one year ago, I was the most dreaded outcast of this family—a divorced un-Christian. And now I was walking through a snowstorm to bring communion to Gretchen's mother on her last Christmas.

Back home, Ray, Gretchen's father, had prepared the kitchen table with a white cloth, a small wooden cross, and a single white candle. As I faced this thin, tearful woman, I realized I loved her. The atmosphere in the kitchen became reverent as Gretchen and her sisters knelt on the hard floor and Ray lit the candle. I was aware of the great faith and love of this family and in a way I felt unworthy to be the one bringing the host. It was indeed a blessing for me.

We all said the Our Father, then I held up the host and said, "This is the Lamb of God who takes away the sins of the world. Happy are we who are called to this supper." I gave it to the frail woman and prayed, "May the body of Christ bring you everlasting life." As we concluded, knowing it wasn't the usual protocol, I gave her a kiss.

As I returned to the church I was aware that I had been allowed to perform this act by the grace of God. And perhaps, in the process, Father O'Brien had been introduced to the lay ministry.

This situation has been a great lesson for me. I pray that should my own daughter come to me with a boyfriend or potential husband, I will pause and look for the good in him, instead of singling out his faults. I can see now that he could end up bringing me communion as I near my own death. For this is how Christ works—from where you least expect him, he comes.

After calling my children and wishing them a merry Christmas, I was moved to write this prayer for Christmas dinner:

> Father, before giving thanks for this beautiful meal, we reflect on Christmas. In the distant past, the Romans gathered during this time in December to celebrate the "Festival of Lights." Christians developed this into the celebration of the light of our life, Jesus, your son, whom you gave to us.
>
> Father, we thank you for your gift to us, and this opportunity to share our Christmas together in your presence. Bring to each one of us the courage to follow your will in our times of difficulty just as your son did in his most difficult times. We pray for those less fortunate than ourselves at this time, and thank you for your many gifts to us. Let us now enjoy this meal, knowing you are truly the light of our life.
>
> In memory of your son, Jesus Christ. Amen.

Chapter 10

In the desert

Friday, January 12, 1979

For the past week everyone has been throwing up on me. In Las Vegas I had just completed my presentation on the psychiatric aspects of headache and walked into a bathroom when some oaf came barging through the door and vomited all over my back. As he stumbled off to the commode, I turned and looked at the back of my coat, covered with little chunks and pieces of unmentionable debris, not to mention the floor, the mirror, and one of my shoes. I was a sight, and smelled worse. My colleagues laughed for the next three days but I still do not see the humor in it.

Yesterday I returned to the hospital. My first consult was with a man in the ICU who had had a stroke. He was in terrible shape because it had affected his dominant hemisphere and he was unable to speak. As I carefully prodded him with my pin to check for sensory involvement, he turned toward me and suddenly projected a stream of yellow vomit in an arc right above my head. I scampered a few feet away to safe territory and checked; I couldn't see any spots. Just as I was congratulating myself for my fast footwork I noticed my black bag, sitting on the table near his bedside, covered with reeking yellow stuff. This time the nurses seemed to see some tremendous humor in the situation but they stopped smiling when I asked them if they would please clean up the mess.

Later I went up to the medical ward to see a woman with a headache. She was a plump, unhappy soul who complained of great pain even as I touched the bedrail. When I asked her to open her mouth I didn't expect her to gag. She did, though, lunging at me at the same time. I cowered against the curtain, trying to protect both myself and my bag. This time nothing came except wave after wave of dry heaves. Finally she recovered some composure and I managed to do the same, cautiously completing my exam.

Somewhere I remember hearing something about "glory" in medicine. Well, this is it. I must say that at times spiritual life isn't much better. Tonight begins another diaconate training weekend.

Sunday evening, January 14, 1979

The weekend seemed different this time. The greetings and the atmosphere were more subdued; fewer wives and children were present, and some of our youthful enthusiasm seems to have waned. We sat there, hour after hour, listening to our instructors, taking notes, and drinking coffee to stay awake. The novelty has worn off. I think we are becoming aware that this is one weekend a month of long hours and hard work. Mine was also cluttered with thoughts of missing Gretchen (she is visiting her mother in Pennsylvania) and anxiety about my impending oral neurology board exams.

The lectures continue to be of the highest caliber. Father Reardon spoke on Paul's Epistles to the Galatians and Romans. I enjoyed the information on baptism (Romans 6). As Father Reardon expressed it: "In other words, when we were baptized we went into the tomb with Jesus and joined him in death, so that as Christ was raised from the dead by the Father's glory, we too might live a new life." The key is how we too might "live a new life"—he didn't say we would automatically be raised to glory as Christ was. We don't earn salvation. It is given to us by the Father, and we must live the life we are given, the bad along with the good.

We had two new instructors, Monsignor Poe, who spoke for three hours on sacramental theology, and Monsignor Burns, who talked to us about spirituality and prayer. Fausto gave us two excellent hours on liturgy: planning, preparation, and execution. I found helpful his constant reminder that when we work with priests who are not too eager to associate with us, we should always remember "humility, tact, and love."

The most exciting lectures were by Monsignor Burns, an elderly retired priest who sparkles with a calm spirituality. He started out explaining that we can't be taught how to pray; we have to do it. Unless we seek, we will not find. He said we have to learn that God is present everywhere. If we become aware of his "here and nowness," we can always talk to him. If our thoughts dry up (which they will), we can say a Jesus prayer: "Lord Jesus, son of the living God, be merciful to me, for I have sinned." He told us not to get hung up about sin but to be concerned about our motives. We should not forget the gifts God has given us, or that we are supposed to use them. To begin to know the heart and mind of Jesus we must pray and read the scriptures, over and over again. We must make time for him to work with us. I like his message. If we talk with God, answers will be coming, but not necessarily overnight.

The hardest part of Monsignor Burns's advice was that we should try to pray an hour a day, and if we have trouble finding an hour, then we should spend two! And here I am, Russ Packard, M.D. and S.M. (Spiritual Midget). I honestly think I'm great if I spend five minutes a day in prayer. I must try to give more time to my God, and let him have some more time with me.

Monday, January 15, 1979

I find giving so difficult. I don't understand how God could want me to join his small army. I hoard money. I extend my hand at the "kiss of peace" during the training weekend while the others kiss and embrace. I try to avoid work so I can go lie on the beach; and my prayer time with God is between two and five minutes a day.

Even at this moment I am aware that I could go up to the little hospital chapel and be with God for a time, but my mind is cluttered with thoughts of making rounds, answering telephone calls, and preparing lectures and papers. What am I doing with my life?

I just finished reading *Beyond Death's Door* by Dr. Maurice Rawlings. Some people he resuscitated from clinical "death" were able to recall experiences of leaving their bodies and ascending (or descending in some cases) to different places, some pleasant, some not. Many "good" Christians descended. I may be in for the "great black lake of fire," as one person described it. I just don't feel that I can give.

Wednesday, January 17, 1979

This morning I reached out to Jesus for the first time. This statement may sound strange. I have long been aware of how I have directed all my prayers to "God." I have often included Jesus, but it has been more "lip service" than anything else. I finally let my feelings out. I was angry at Jesus, jealous, hateful. I resented him for being "special." Why was he picked? Why not me? I really lashed out at him. I felt pretty small when I finished sounding off, but I realized (as he did all along) that all this emotion had to come out for me to grow to know him. While I had always respected him, I never wanted to talk to him.

This morning I needed to talk to him because he is tangible. He knows what it's like to be human. Last night Gretchen and I talked about having a baby. I have a great deal of anxiety about it; my past is emotionally stacked against me. On the surface my previous marriage broke up over the issue of "another baby." The question was much deeper, though, reflecting an attitude of "either I submit, or the marriage will break up." Sure enough, when I resisted, the marriage folded.

Since then my feelings about a baby have changed. Gretchen allowed me time to heal, and her prayers asked God's aid in my healing. This morning I reached out to Jesus to help me continue to grow. I hope he can forgive me for the way I feel about him. Perhaps he wanted me to be aware of these things, so I could come to know him better.

Saturday, January 20, 1979

Last night we had our local diaconate meeting. For the first fifteen minutes I sat there in a daze, thinking I would rather be any place else. For another fifteen minutes we all talked about nothing.

The topic then moved to the sacraments. We were all annoyed at our sacramental theology teacher who had come to the weekend obviously ill-prepared. Then I questioned infant baptism. For a half-hour Fausto and I hurled our opinions across the room at each other. I accused most priests of "giving tickets out of limbo" rather than offering infant baptism as a sacrament, or as the initiation of a new member into the Christian community. (I was directing my remarks at the people who do not go to church but bring their babies in for "the ritual.")

Fausto said it isn't right to judge the faith of others. By offering baptism he has a chance to talk with the parents and he will at least see the child again for communion and confirmation. We never settled anything. I finally gave up when another candidate said I would be punishing innocent children by refusing them baptism. At the end of the meeting, Fausto was all smiles and gave me a kiss. He loves a hassle.

Monday, January 22, 1979

Gretchen's mother is holding on by a thread to the last of this temporary life we have. Gretchen and I are living day by day right now, waiting for the phone to ring with the news of her death.

Terry Wilson returned from Bethesda this week. He came in with his wife the other day; they have decided to remain here in Florida. I offered to continue following him as a patient. He looks good. He's wearing a gray stocking cap to cover his scarred and barren head. Surgery and radiation to the head act like a devastating forest fire—there is nothing left when it's over. Fortunately Terry's exam showed that he is essentially normal and his spirits are fair. He is planning to go back to work for a month before he is medically retired. The big question is whether he will be allowed to wear the cap, instead of his military hat. I told him to wear it, and see what happens. Occasionally even the navy bends.

I mentioned to Terry and his wife that I was following another patient who had a similar tumor. He was treated with radiation and surgery and he is still stable three and a half years after his surgery. They sat up in their chairs with widened eyes and responded in unison, "Really?" I think they were infused with new hope, and I believe it is real. Somehow I know I will be with Terry through this ordeal.

In a way I'm surprised that he is back but in another way I'm not. Our lives are linked together, and God is very much in the middle. I may not always understand God, but I can sense his presence in this relationship.

Sunday morning, January 28, 1979

Gretchen's mother died last night. After hearing the news, Gretchen and I held each other and cried. Yet we were also relieved. Her suffering is over now. She passed away peacefully at home with the family kneeling at her bedside. I cannot imagine a more beautiful way to die. Both Gretchen and I reflected on the countless number of patients we have seen who have died alone, without any dignity, surrounded only by monitors and machines, IV tubing, a doctor who wants to get back to bed, and a nurse who wants to get her paperwork done.

We were caught in an awkward situation. I was supposed to leave for a board review course in neurology in Miami and Gretchen had been planning to come along. We decided it would be better if I went on by myself and she returned to Pennsylvania. After the course I will fly up to be with her and the family.

Saturday morning, February 3, 1979

Last night I was officially installed by Bishop Gracida as a candidate to the diaconate and an acolyte at the cathedral. An acolyte assists the priest and can distribute the sacred eucharist to the community of the faithful and to the sick. It was a beautiful liturgy and again I was moved by the dynamic presence of Bishop Gracida. His dark piercing eyes were confident and inspiring. Eight priests (including Pat) concelebrated the mass but another group of priests sat at the back of the cathedral, in what amounted to a silent protest of the return of permanent deacons to the Church. I wish they could see that we are only here to help them, not to threaten them or take away their ministry. We are the least of all ministers, yet we are looked upon with scorn.

As I reflect on the actual ceremony I feel very pleased. It was not a large or spectacular one, but very simple, quite fitting for what we will ultimately be. During communion, the men distributed the eucharist to their families in a very touching moment.

I was aware as all this was happening that I was a bit out of it from my travels. I had arrived from the board review course in Miami just an hour before, and raced starving to Pat's apartment. We had to leave immediately with the dinner still in the oven. By ten o'clock I was hungry as a crocodile and we ate the dried, overcooked chicken as if it were a great feast.

Then I had to go to the hospital and leave word that I was checking out on emergency leave. Piles of consults were taped to my door, to the point that I could hardly find the doorknob, but they will just have to wait another few days. I went home to unpack, feed the cat, repack, and head back to the airport for my flight to Pennsylvania.

I am scribbling this now on the plane. I still have not caught up with myself but I am certainly looking forward to being with my Gretchen again. I have been too long without her.

We are nearly in Pittsburgh. I can see patches of snow on the ground. For the past hour I have been reading *Interpreting the Miracles* by R. H. Fuller, an enlightening book. We so often misinterpret the meaning of a miracle, forgetting that the healing of the blind often symbolizes the opening of our eyes to faith. We also at times feel discouraged when a healing does not occur instantly but rather over a period of time in a completely natural way. God works this way through history and nature, slowly. I am beginning to feel that the more I learn, the less I know. As small parts unfold, the mystery seems to deepen.

Monday, February 5, 1979

Considering the recent death, all is relatively peaceful here. We all know that Betty does not have to suffer any more and we know where she is now. It's almost exciting to think about it. I find myself wondering how frightening death must be to those who simply die, with no hope of anything more. Of course we grieve and fight to cling to our physical life. We are human; we cannot help having these feelings.

Gretchen's little sister, Bridget, who is only ten, expressed her feelings in a beautiful way. After her mother died, she looked down at the lifeless body and said, "You know, she was like a present, all gift-wrapped. But the present was inside the box, and now that part is gone, leaving just an empty box."

We must die to rise again.

Sunday evening, February 11, 1979

The last thing I feel like doing right now is writing. I see no point to it, except that it will show what a pain it is to be a Christian. I feel as if I'm in the desert.

Gretchen and I returned from snowy Pennsylvania Thursday night and I went back to work Friday. I was greeted by two weeks of EEGs, angry patients, a pile of administrative garbage, and news that my paper on headache had been accepted for publication, but rejected for the award for best paper. I was disappointed about that.

We then went rushing out Friday night for another training weekend. We got our church history tests back as soon as we walked in the door. I got a B+. I was disappointed; I wanted an A! Father Nass, perfectionist that he is, gave only one A. So I can't complain too much—especially since I haven't been a Catholic for even a year yet. Later I learned that four men hadn't turned in a paper at all!

Our lectures were good this weekend. Father Reardon finished his series on Paul and plans to start the synoptic Gospels next month. Monsignor Burns came back to deliver three more hours on spirituality. He was very practical again, speaking about the importance of being reflective before mass and on ways to avoid distractions in prayer. Then we had more lectures on liturgy, social ministry, and youth ministry.

Even though I appreciated the lectures, my emotions were diving lower and lower with each passing hour. Father Reardon announced that he was going to be giving an exam on Paul and it was the straw that broke the camel's back. I was absolutely overwhelmed. I skipped our next class and paced my room, fearing my overloaded hospital schedule and my upcoming neurology board exam for which I haven't yet had time to study. I felt that my prayer life was nonexistent and began to question why I was in this program. I tried to bury my feelings by reading a cheap paperback but it didn't help.

Finally I went down the hall and knocked at Fausto's door. He answered, wearing his ever-present smile, but it vanished when he saw my face. I unloaded on him. We talked for an hour. I went through all that was on my mind and for the first time I talked about Pat's leaving. I almost cried. Pat is my support and my main source of spiritual direction. I felt that I couldn't go on without him. My emotional outburst brought on a migraine and I slid even lower in my chair, covering my eyes. Fausto offered to do what he could to help with my spiritual direction but he is obviously limited because of his own involvement in the program and all the running around he does in our large diocese. I thought then of Monsignor Burns as a possible replacement, because I enjoyed his approach to prayer and spirituality. Fausto suggested I talk with him.

After I finally wound down (about 10:00 p.m.) I met with Monsignor Leo Burns in his room and we talked for an hour. He retired about a year ago and felt that God wasn't finished with him for some reason, so after a few months he came back into service. He said he would be delighted to pick up as my director after Pat leaves. I feel comfortable about that, although no one will ever replace Pat for me.

Tuesday, February 13, 1979

I was meditating today when suddenly I was saying to Jesus that I hate him and his humanness. I didn't feel any guilt, only a strange sort of encouragement to continue to search for the roots of my hatred. I don't understand it. This past weekend Monsignor Burns had asked me if I felt any hatred. Surprised, I told him I frequently get angry, but I don't hate. Then this morning I suddenly found myself hating Jesus. Great choice. Up to my neck in trouble again.

I continued to meditate on my hate. I was irritated that Jesus is special and I'm not. He is great. My paper gets rejected. He performs miracles. I get a B+. He prays for hours; I can't pray for more than a few minutes. He carries everyone's burdens and sins; I can't even hold myself up. He died on the cross, and now he's sharing the damn thing with me. Me! He is filled with love and I am filled with hate. He seduced me into this life and I was foolish enough to follow. And now look at me—he's making me look at myself. And I hate what I see.

Wednesday, February 14, 1979

At mass, Pat asked Brad and me to break the homemade bread and distribute it to the people, explaining that we were now acolytes within the diocese and this service was part of our function. If only other priests would do this, lay ministry wouldn't be such a shock to the people. Half the time they think we are committing sin if we distribute communion.

After mass Pat and I finally talked about his leaving. Several times my eyes filled with tears as I expressed how much I would miss him. I wish he weren't going, but I know it has to be. He was pleased that Monsignor Burns is to be my new spiritual director. We chatted about our early talks, the diaconate training program, Kübler-Ross, fundamentalists, and came back to ourselves. He thought it might all come crashing down on him some day in Cuba when he is meditating quietly. We have both grown so much together.

Tuesday evening, February 27, 1979

I walked into a neurologic disaster this morning. When I arrived at the hospital I found a note on my door asking me to review an EEG and do a consultation as soon as possible on an eighteen-month-old baby boy who had nearly drowned and then been resuscitated. I looked at his EEG and it was terribly slow and suppressed. Sometimes I feel that the neurologist is the grim reaper of the hospital.

I went up to the wards to make rounds and stopped to spend fifteen minutes of prayer in the chapel. I had just settled down when a couple came in and sat two rows in front of me. I heard them whisper something about an EEG and I knew instantly they were the child's parents. I had not seen their son yet and they did not realize I was his neurologist. I felt awkward, yet I knew we were all in the chapel for the same reason. I prayed for their son and for them. They walked out silently holding hands. My fifteen minutes were not up but I decided to leave and evaluate the child.

Young David See had blond curls and a little diaper around his mid-section. He also had IV's, a nasotracheal tube, arterial lines, monitors, and patches over his eyes. There was evidence of brainstem function in that he was still breathing and had roving eye movements but there was no response to pain or recognition of his name. He had not changed significantly since he was admitted earlier this morning.

Judging from the exam and the EEG I had to tell his parents the prognosis for any meaningful recovery was remote, but I could not be sure until I repeated another EEG and continued to follow him over the next few days. They stood in silence and in tears while I wondered what this suffering was all about. Since leaving them, I have called on God over and over to help this child. I know he has heard but I don't know what he will do. I can do nothing.

Is this yet another desert? Is baby David a young cactus in the desert that will never bloom? As a neurologist I do not foresee a recovery, but as a spiritual fool I continue to hope, and to pray.

Ash Wednesday, February 28, 1979

I just got back from helping Pat with mass and the distribution of the ashes, making the sign of the cross on foreheads. Pat asked those who think this is "the little ritual of the Church that we should do," to stay in their pews rather than be hypocrites. He wanted people to be aware of the symbolism: from dust we came, to dust we shall return. We are simply dust in the wind of life. I don't know how many stayed in their pews because I was making a mess of dabbing the ashes on foreheads. From the altar one could pick out my crosses from all the rest—black smudges, without form, one of which was on Pat's forehead.

Little David See's mother was at mass. I made a special effort to reach her at the sign of peace, and again at the end of mass when I went up to her and asked how she was. Troubled, tired eyes looked back into mine. She didn't have the energy to reply—she just shook her head. I told her I wanted her to know that my prayers were with her. She looked back at me with what seemed like hate. I felt suddenly awkward as if I had overstepped somewhere. Perhaps it was difficult for her to hear words of prayer from the same man who had given her such grim news about her son. I certainly didn't mean to hurt her in any way or to make excuses. I can't change the EEG; I can only read it, and pray that it changes tomorrow.

Friday, March 2, 1979

The damn EEG is the same as it was two days ago. In some ways it is almost worse than being flat. Taking everything into consideration, the outlook is awful. There is little hope for more than a heart beating in a vegetable. Without using the same language I explained the situation to the parents, who stood there in horror.

All this bleakness does not mean I have given up. I do find myself feeling a tension, though, between my medical training and my infant spirituality. Even though my neurologic reasoning tells me there is little hope of meaningful brain recovery, I still hope, because I believe that it could happen. At times I think and speak like a physician, at times like a religious person, and at other times like a fool. A fool is probably closest to the truth.

I have been flogged enough this week by the hospital. I think I'm going to leave a little early so I can get ready for the training weekend.

Sunday afternoon, March 4, 1979

Well, here it is Lent and you-know-who ate a steak on Friday. I don't think I will ever learn.

I should have known from the beginning that trouble was brewing. I arrived at the hotel early Friday afternoon after a leisurely drive down the coast, but while I was checking into my room I accidentally dropped my hat into the commode and the eagle fell off again. I keep trying to tell the navy that I was never meant to wear a hat. Maybe they will believe me now.

I settled into a cozy seat by the window in the hotel dining room, overlooking the bay. When my steak arrived I was watching a group of seagulls flapping around outside the window and the sun beginning to set. I felt a warm glow inside. Suddenly, after my first bite, I realized it is Lent and we aren't supposed to eat meat on

Fridays. I sat there looking down at my juicy steak, glanced over my shoulder to make sure that none of my colleagues was around, and decided to be a sinning hypocrite and continue my dinner. What can I say?

Fausto, our lovable Italian priest, began the evening with two more hours on moral theology. When he said he characterized himself as an expert on sin, I felt better about my steak.

Actually he did a good job on some sensitive topics, including sexuality. He said that we are created in God's image, including our sexuality which makes possible love and union in marriage. And love is mentioned again and again in the Bible. For a few seconds my thoughts expanded and I thought that by studying "us" we can learn more about God. Sometimes the complexity of the body is incredible, yet it is also simple, living, and creative.

Saturday was stormy all day. Father Reardon's cigarettes got wet and I thought he would try to smoke the chalk. Finally he borrowed someone else's, saying he didn't think he could read Greek without them. He spent four hours on a comparison of the synoptic Gospels (Matthew, Mark, and Luke).

Although several teachers were not able to make the weekend because of the storm, Bishop Gracida managed to come and speak to us. He is an incredibly moving person. At one point he asked us to "risk everything" because the program has to change. He said St. Leo College will begin to give us college credit for our courses, by extension. We have the opportunity now for a bachelor's degree in religious studies, but the arrangements are still in the early stages and very uncertain. After he finished speaking, many of us had questions and reservations, but there wasn't one of us who would not follow him. It isn't just his leadership; we can feel the Spirit moving in our program. It's alive in us. There are no charges to the candidates yet our program has paid for itself. We all make donations for the rooms and the meals, and at the conclusion of every weekend somehow all the bills are paid.

On Sunday morning we had a lecture on sacramental theology and practical aspects of the rites of baptism and confirmation. There was further discussion about youth ministry, the new catechism, and catechesis (teaching the Catholic faith). Sometimes we try to cram the Bible down our children's throats before they have the capacity to digest it, or even an appetite for it. Then we stop teaching them in the sixth or eighth grade and wonder why so many turn away from the Church in their late teens, when we have "raised them so well."

Monday, March 12, 1979

Little David See's EEG is slower and more suppressed. I had to tell the pediatricians and his family that I did not expect any meaningful recovery. Coming from a neurologist that news usually means what it says. He is also getting pneumonia now and will probably succumb to it.

Tuesday, March 13, 1979

David See died today. When I told Gretchen she said it was probably a blessing. I hadn't thought of it that way but I suppose it is. Every time I see a child die I feel that I die a little. The past few weeks have indeed been a desert experience.

Chapter 11

Struggles, failures, goodbyes

Wednesday, March 14, 1979

I continue to struggle with daily prayer. During the week I go to the small hospital chapel and sit in the semi-darkness before making rounds. Actually I don't sit. I twitch. From the moment I am there I start to squirm like a child at a boring movie. My mind fills up with patients, rounds, EEGs to read, and places I have to be.

Despite all of these temptations I make myself stay for a full fifteen minutes. Some of the random thoughts and urges begin to subside after a few minutes; sometimes they continue for the entire time. Occasionally I pick up a copy of the Gospels and read a few lines of scripture. It helps me to unwind and put myself in God's presence. He must be delighted to have a few minutes with this bit of irritable protoplasm he created.

At other times I put the fifteen minutes off until the end of the day. When I delay, I invariably lose. It is important for me to pray early in the morning.

Struggles, failures, goodbyes

Thursday, March 15, 1979

I am wondering again why I am writing this. At times I feel that I was given a start and then abandoned. I don't know when or if I am in touch with God's presence anymore. When I first started to write and pray it seemed so easy. It was clear and beautiful—inspired, I thought. Now I feel awkward, unsure of myself, and unsure of who God is. At times I feel I am only going through a series of motions, traveling nowhere.

Thursday, March 22, 1979

There are whispers about the hospital that I am a "religious fanatic." The hospital is a small world for gossip and a few of the nurses have told Gretchen that some of the doctors think I am a bit crazy. As I understand it, I am a fanatic because I am "always giving lectures and weird things like that." I have even been "seen in the chapel" before rounds. I find the name-calling rather amusing and in some ways I can understand it, because I used to call people religious nuts if they showed even the slightest interest in faith, or went to church with any regularity. I remember laughing at "all that nonsense" so I don't mind being called a fanatic at this point. I do hope I am never accused of trying to force religion on anyone.

In the same vein, last weekend my mother accused me of being mean and uncaring for refusing to give her medicine to control her blood sugar now that she is diabetic. I used to give her a few samples of medicine for stomachaches, sore throats, and so on, but I don't feel comfortable prescribing medication for diabetes since I don't treat it. I have advised her to get her own doctor in town. So, I am not only a fanatic; I am also mean.

Friday, March 23, 1979

Terry Wilson and his wife came to see me yesterday with his latest head scan. It didn't look too bad compared to the scan done prior to his surgery and radiation therapy. But the procedures he has been through also present a problem: I can't tell now what is tumor, radiation effect, or post-surgical effect. I explained that things looked pretty good and showed them the difference in the scans. The scan will have to be repeated in six months for comparison.

As we were finishing up, his wife commented that they were "just trusting the Lord." I finally broke my vow of not speaking to patients about God. I told them that I too had been praying for him to be well. They were both very touched. I can see it now; pretty soon I will be accused of being both a fanatic and a faith healer.

My mother and I have not talked since our explosion over the weekend. Another thing that set me off was her insistence that Gretchen was influencing me "to be so different." Also, Gretchen had "made me go into the Church." Those statements made me furious but I chose to let them roll off my back. I know I will never convince my parents that I entered the Church freely.

Thursday, March 29, 1979

This week has been so hectic that I have missed a couple of days' prayer and was unable to attend mass on Wednesday.

Tuesday night a curious thing happened in chapel. I was stuck at the hospital working from 4:00 until 10:00 in the evening walk-in clinic. At one point I felt that I was going to start screaming if I saw another child with a runny nose. I was tempted to throw a fit in the emergency room and tell the navy I couldn't take any more general practice (after all I am a specialist), and they could take their damn walk-ins and shove them up their caboose. Instead of doing that, however, I decided to take a break and go up to the chapel for a few minutes.

When I arrived there I was not in the mood to talk with anyone. My head was pounding from the strain of nonstop patients since early morning. I noticed a rather long-haired young man wearing a hospital robe and stretched out lengthwise in the pew two rows in front of me. As I sat down he gave me a friendly smile and started to stare at me. I bowed my head and began my prayer: "Turkeys and crocks, turkeys and crocks. That's all you give me." Obviously the prayer was not going well so I looked up. My "friend" was still staring at me. He asked if I wanted to talk about anything. I wanted to tell him to leave me alone, but I said, "No," and bowed my head again. A few minutes passed silently. For some reason I found myself praying earnestly for him. I wanted to help myself, but there I was reaching out although I felt I didn't have an ounce to give.

When I looked up again we started to talk. At first I was evasive and turned things around so he talked about himself. He had come to the chapel because he had made a pass at another man's wife that day. He felt very guilty about it because it was not the first time that he had done such a thing. He said that just before I came in, he had talked with a woman in the chapel and he somehow felt forgiven. Then I told him about my frustrations: I had arrived at the hospital earlier in the day and found four consults on my desk. I always try to do all my consults the day that I receive them, but having to work in the walk-in clinic disrupted my plans. I notified the ward that I would not be able to do two of the consults until the following day. After I had made the call I felt a mixture of pleasure and guilt. I was also angry that I was expected to be everywhere at once. The young patient said he thought what I had done was "just human." Even Jesus wasn't able to take care of everyone during his time on earth though he did more for the world than any other human. Sometimes we have to say no, he concluded.

After the patient left, I sat and reflected how my attitude with him was very much in character. I am basically unpleasant. I went grumbling and growling into the chapel wanting to talk to God while ignoring his people. I went to get away from men and women with problems and met a bearded stranger with another problem. Yet this very person whom I wanted to reject, even started to reject, was Christ-like in the way he gave of himself to comfort me. Christ was right there in front of me, yet I didn't see him. At that moment we were two equal humans. There was no officer-enlisted man gap, no doctor-patient differences—just two men struggling together in the presence of Christ.

Sunday, April 1, 1979

Friday night Gretchen and I headed down to Destin for another training weekend. This time I was lying in the back seat, trying to forget about my migraine. It came on as I arrived home Friday afternoon so I went to bed for a half-hour, hoping it would go away. For the first time in my life I held onto my rosary beads and stumbled my way through the rosary. My headache didn't go away and I thought of skipping the entire weekend but Gretchen said she would drive so I crawled into the back seat. When we arrived I was still not able to pull myself together so I went to bed, skipping the classes.

On Saturday morning I was feeling better, but tortured with mixed feelings about what I should be doing. My board exam was just a week away, so after Father Reardon's scripture classes I went to my room to study pediatric neurology for three hours. By that time my headache had returned and it was time for dinner.

Our community meal was hot dogs and beans. Every month the quality seems to deteriorate. Several families had brought their children, who were sitting happily in all the chairs. I felt like grabbing the little brats and flinging them out the window. Gretchen and I sat on the floor. I walked away swearing I would never eat with the community again.

Back in the classroom I was asked to do a reading and I snapped back that I didn't feel like it. The poor soul who had asked me was a bit taken aback. He asked me if he could pray for me. I gave him a sarcastic smile. I felt like a real animal. I was at the end of the my rope. How could prayer help me?

I don't know whether or not it helped but he never reassigned the reading and when the time came I got out of my seat and read:

> Love is patient; love is kind. Love is not jealous, it does not put on airs, it is not snobbish. Love is never rude, it is not self-seeking, it is not prone to anger; neither does it brood over injuries. Love does not rejoice in what is wrong but rejoices with the truth. There is no limit to love's forbearance, to its trust, its hope, its power to endure. Love never fails. There are in the end three things that last: faith, hope and love and the greatest of these is love.
> (1 Corinthians, 13: 4-13)

Even though I am far from loving, I am surrounded by love.

Tuesday, April 3, 1979

The movie *Jesus of Nazareth* is on TV this week. It is a film conceived and made with love, maintaining a beautiful balance between religious fervor and realism. Gretchen and I have shared a meal with Pat each night and watched the movie together. Pat brought a loaf of bread he had made, which tasted as if it had a monk's robe in it, and Gretchen (thank God) made a casserole. We definitely could not live on bread alone.

Thursday, April 5, 1979

I saw Jesus yesterday in the most unusual place. As I was leaving the hospital I was paged to see a patient in the emergency room. I always become irritated when I am paged as I am leaving and this time I was called to see a dirty, seedy old veteran not eligible for care at our hospital. He smelled awful, had grass and dirt smeared all over his dirty clothes, a pockmarked face and a somewhat alcoholic, disagreeable disposition. He had just had a seizure. The internist asked me to "look him over quickly so we can transfer him." What a joke. There is no way to look over a patient who could have anything from a subdural hematoma to an electrolyte imbalance in a few minutes. I was tired and I felt as if I were being called to see a troll who had been hauled up from under a bridge.

I started my exam reluctantly, not even wanting to touch his grimy skin. Suddenly I became aware that this poor creature was another human, lowly and broken, the perfect shadow for Christ to hide in. I spoke gently to the man and a tear formed in the corner of his eye. I hoped he understood me. He wouldn't or couldn't talk and then he had another seizure. We started him on anticonvulsants and transferred him to another hospital. I had approached this man as "less than a man;" I had even joked with the internist about him. I am sorry.

Friday, April 6, 1979

I have been fairly successful the past few days at getting into the chapel and staying there for fifteen minutes. But I can't believe the struggle I have been having there.

I have had to learn to sit in God's presence more than to pray. I have been (and still am) struggling between my human attachments and the spiritual aspects of my life. When I arrive in the chapel, I start to think of all the other things I should be doing, like picking up my mail, getting gas for the car, and making a phone call—all those things so important to everyday life. I must learn to set these earthly chores aside for a few minutes so I can sit in the presence of God. Jesus often went off alone to pray. This is something I must learn to do, but first I have to become comfortable with myself.

When I finally settle into prayer I find myself facing another problem. I cannot find God. He is so elusive. Or is it I who am elusive? I struggle to give him fifteen minutes of my day while expecting him always to be there. Somehow I believe he really is. The only problem is that he seems to live in the shadows. It's like being in a forest and having the feeling that someone else is there, lurking quietly behind a large tree. I talk to this presence in the shadows, beg him to show himself, and the silence seems to deepen; the darkness grows. Then when I least expect it, he pops into the sunlight of a clearing for a moment. I blink in astonishment and then he is gone again.

Monday, April 9, 1979

I am at the Marriott Hotel in New Orleans waiting to take my oral exams in neurology tomorrow morning. I have never spent more time on my knees. I have been praying in an almost desperate way to pass the boards and be rid of them. Pass or fail, however, I do feel that I am not alone here.

Tuesday, April 17, 1979

I have not written in over a week because of my discouragement. The day of my board exam was a true experience in humility. I began early with a prayer, dedicating my day and my efforts to God. I could no longer see any personal reason for taking the boards. I had already been through psychiatry exams and the written exams in neurology, and now the orals. But I gave everything I had and was totally spent at the conclusion. One of the hours went very badly. I may not have passed. I was so discouraged I have not felt like writing or doing much of anything since.

Tuesday, April 24, 1979

I failed my hour of child neurology. I did pass the two hours of adult neurology so I have only to repeat the child hour. I am rescheduled for October in Chicago. If I had failed the entire exam I think I would have given the whole process up but with one hour left it's like a damn carrot dangling on a string in front of me. I don't feel so bad as I thought I would, but I certainly don't feel good.

Wednesday, April 25, 1979

This is Gretchen's last week in the navy; her four-year obligation is over. My time will be up next year. We have decided to stay here in Pensacola and are looking at a new waterfront house. I have an offer to enter private practice when I get out of the the navy and I think I may accept it. I would really like to stay here and continue my training in the diaconate program.

Thursday, April 26, 1979

I talked with Pat yesterday about all that is happening. I feel that I can't see the forest for the trees. I told him I felt as if I were pulling away from my spiritual life with all the excitement and change of a new house and possible private practice. He said I am right in the middle of my spiritual life. Our flesh is not separate from our spirit. If our "fleshly" yearnings make a wrong choice, the spirit doesn't pack its bags and leave; it comes along and is always there, wherever we are.

Wednesday, May 2, 1979

Unfortunately, pain is part of being alive. The time of Pat's leaving is approaching relentlessly. Yesterday he dropped me off to pick up my car and as I started to get out he said, "Russ, I love you." I almost broke down. Even now my eyes are filling with tears as I write these words. I love him so much. Wednesday afternoon will not be the same without Pat. I have started to do a half-day of private practice to fill up that void.

Sunday, May 6, 1979

During this training weekend I felt like a wild man. If God's message to me was "Ishmael," then being a wild ass of a man certainly fits.

I tried again to go through the rosary on Saturday morning with the group but finally I slipped out the back door. I apologized to Mary and Fausto and sat alone on the back steps in the early morning sunshine. I felt like a misfit. I tried to pray and after a while, Fausto came out and sat down next to me and gave me a hug. I love him.

Later, we had a half-hour for private meditation and I ended up making love to Gretchen. As I hurried back to the classroom I found several of my colleagues down on their knees in front of the altar, praying their hearts out. I felt like an ass. At least we have *some* spiritual men in the class.

As the weekend drew to a close we had another half-hour of public meditation. Some of the men stood up in front of the class and made readings while the others listened in prayerful silence. I leaned over, resting my elbows on my knees, and the next thing I knew I lurched violently and almost fell out of my chair. I had fallen asleep. If God wants *me* for a minister, believe me, there is hope for us all.

Monday, May 14, 1979

Pat leaves in two days. Yesterday, Mother's Day, he said his last mass. Instead of standing with him at the altar, I was back in the pew where I had started. I would have been there with him but I was coughing and sneezing so much I decided to excuse myself. He celebrated with Father Dawson and his new replacement, a rather conservative Irish priest who has been transferred here from the Middle Ages.

During mass my mind was full of memories: my first mass, the first time I accepted the bread and wine, baptism, confirmation, long talks about this mystery we call faith, and actually standing next to Pat at the altar.

After communion Pat handed out long-stemmed roses to the mothers, and the priests blessed them from the altar. Earlier Pat had asked Gretchen to come up at that time (this past week we learned she is pregnant), but she stayed in the pew. I whispered that she had better go up to the altar or Pat would call her. Just as she said, "He wouldn't," his voice drifted down from the altar, "Gretchen, Mrs. Packard, come up here." When she went up Pat gave her two roses. Later, she asked why he had given her two and he replied because he wanted to.

In a way it was fitting that I sat with the people yesterday. I can see the beginning of my own separation from where Pat has taken me. I feel like a new, floundering disciple, or a vice president after the president leaves office. If I stay on here at the naval chapel, I will stagnate and hold onto the past. I have to move on now, too.

I feel an almost unconscious calling to make myself available to the Holy Spirit parish, with Monsignors Burns and Poe. Father Burns will be my new spiritual director, and Father Poe is an exceptionally bright but low key sort of pastor. In some ways that is good because I can't think of anyone who is more low key (dull, in other words) than I am.

Tomorrow night Pat, Gretchen, and I will be getting together for the last time. My God, how Pat has touched us! My prayers are with him; I know he will touch others. He is a true man of God.

Wednesday, May 16, 1979

Pat left last night. We had dinner and then talked about love. We reflected on how hard it is to say, "I love you," to those we care about. How difficult it has been for all of us to say those words to our fathers, mothers, and close friends.

I broke down into tears twice, openly. Pat hid behind his endless gift of gab. As I wept and Gretchen sat in silence, Pat chattered like some demented bird; but we both know him, and we know how much he loves us. He left us some beautiful gifts, many that are priceless and intangible, but also a picture, blending the past three popes and John Paul II, symbolic of the force motivating our renewal within the Church. He also left us a plaque and a card which read: "Of all the fine and wonderful things you have done with your beautiful life, the greatest is, you helped me to God. I will spend eternity thanking you."

And this gift came from the one who helped me to find God.

Chapter 12

Sin and spiritual direction

Thursday, May 17, 1979

I hoped this would be a book of revelation but it is turning out to be a book about sin—unfortunately my own.

I spent my first half-day working in private practice today and had a great time. The patients were interesting and I enjoyed having real secretaries help me in the office. (In the navy I answered my own phone and did my own typing.)

I also came face to face with greed when I ordered an EEG on a woman who probably didn't need it. I wanted the interpretation fee. I was also afraid of potential lawsuits in this new world of private practice. Perhaps I was so excited and anxious I went overboard. I must watch that. Prices are already so high I feel guilty anyway.

Sunday, May 20, 1979

I never thought I would become obsessed with sin. I hate even to use the word because it is so misunderstood. I believe we sin when we either move away from God or sever our relationship with God (mortal sin). I am not talking about looking at a short skirt or swearing out loud at a football game. If that were sin I wouldn't have a chance.

I am becoming painfully aware of my own godlessness. Even though I am more aware of what is right and wrong, I keep doing the wrong things. As an example, I notice lately that I hate making rounds at the hospital. I want to zip by, write a note, and collect my twenty dollars. Sometimes I don't even want to see the patients, but when I think I could be in their place, I go in. Actually, I am not sure I make a lot of difference anyway. One patient thought I was the TV repairman.

After rounds today I went into the hospital chapel feeling lost. I sat there twisting my rubber reflex hammer in my hands and staring up at the altar. I felt like a little child, helpless to stop my sinning ways. I need that man hanging on that cross to help me. I can't do it without him. We humans are basically frail and weak. Jesus is right there for me, yet I continue to trip him up in his effort to help.

Tuesday, May 22, 1979

I found myself reflecting today on the time Jesus wrote in the sand. The scribes and pharisees had approached him about a woman who had committed adultery. They had forced him into a complex situation. If he condemned her they would say that he was not merciful. If he released her, he would be acting in contradiction to the sacred law of Moses, which he had come to fulfill. What a dilemma! He leaned over and wrote something on the ground (John 8:6). What he actually wrote, no one knows. But why did he do it at all? Did he simply want to gain time? Perhaps the whole scene twisted his heart, so he lowered his eyes and doodled. Some say he wrote out the sins of the accusers so they might read them. Any of these interpretations is possible, I suppose, but his very act of writing cannot be overlooked. That same finger writing in the dust on the temple floor, in a symbolic sense, also wrote on the tablets of stone on Sinai! Jesus was reminding them of who had written the Law. I'm quite sure the scribes and pharisees didn't grasp his message.

The symbolism of this writing has moved me deeply. Somewhere along the line a disciple must have seen some reason to include it in the gospel, perhaps also without understanding it. At times I write without understanding, but I know what I write has meaning.

Sin and spiritual direction 125

In considering my own difficulties with sin the past several weeks I am moved by the force with which Jesus can confront. "Let the man among you who has no sin be the first to cast a stone." These are not words from an ordinary person. We need the power that can confront with such force to help us with our own sinfulness. We can't do it alone.

Wednesday, May 23, 1979

My daily prayer continues on its rocky course. Lately I feel that I am just sitting in the chapel, doing nothing. I look at Jesus on the cross and wonder where he is. I wonder where I am. I hardly even talk to God. I listen, and hear nothing. Occasionally, others slip in quietly to kneel and cross themselves. The next minute they bless themselves again and silently leave. I wonder what they do in those thirty seconds. I wonder if I should just come in and say, "Hi, God," and leave. Why should I spend fifteen minutes doing nothing?

Sometimes I think prayer must be important simply because of all the interferences I face getting into it. Every time I start to go to the chapel there are a million interruptions. Many times they are too demanding and I veer off my course and head straight for the distraction. Invariably, it is one of these "important" little things that somehow seem meaningless when I think about them for a few minutes.

The fifteen minutes that I spend in chapel are often the longest of my day, like a flight in a balloon over uncharted territory. Most of the flight time is spent in the balloon, listening to the wind. But there are times when I see a beautiful sunrise and the experience is so moving that I want to keep going so I can see another, even if I have to drift the entire night or through a storm. I guess I am waiting for another sunrise. Perhaps I should simply lean back and enjoy the ride, let the wind carry me where it will. I think of all the people who don't have a balloon, or if they do, are too busy or afraid to take the ride.

Thursday, May 24, 1979

Today went by rapidly. I saw Monsignor Burns for my first hour of spiritual direction. What a kind and gentle man! I am going to enjoy meeting with him. I know he can help me grow. As the rain fell outside and the grandfather clock tick-tocked away in the quiet of his study, I found it easy to talk with Monsignor Burns. I wanted to spend all day there, discussing my floundering relationship with God and learning to pray. I am pleased that God has brought us together. It has been important for me on my journey to have a traveling companion, someone who can take me by the hand and gently guide me.

I had a light afternoon in the office with just one new patient and one follow-up. The follow-up was the woman for whom I had felt so foolish ordering an EEG last week. She came in feeling much better, partly because she "felt so reassured when the EEG was normal." Perhaps some of my clinical judgment came through, despite my greed.

Friday evening, May 25, 1979

I stopped by Holy Spirit Church this evening and attended a film on healing. The biggest skeptic in that charismatic audience was myself. I did enjoy the film, however; the concept of healing was presented in a very positive way, as a natural part of Christian ministry, reflecting Jesus' own ministry. Although Jesus called on us to suffer with him as we follow him, he never said anything about physical suffering. In fact, every time he met someone suffering, he tried to help that person. Never did he say, "I want you to carry that burden for me."

I was also impressed that the healings were not usually "miracle" cures. People didn't suddenly jump out of their wheelchairs and run the world's fastest mile. Things moved slowly, very much the way God acts in nature. Often the first thing to occur is the relief of pain. Next, physical disability may be mitigated, and later some actual structural change may occur. Some don't feel anything happen, except that they seem aware of a tremendous feeling of love in the room. The healing team often has to pray twice, or more, or even continuously. It is not just a one time "zapping." (Jesus had to touch the blind man twice on one occasion to fully restore his sight.)

The people in the room viewing the film were very much interested in my thoughts because I am a physician. I said I continued to be skeptical but I admitted there is clearly a place for prayer in patient care.

I was keenly aware of the love in the prayer group following the film, but I found myself holding back. I didn't know the words of the hymns they were singing so I bowed my head and listened. I found myself identifying with Father Poe, who sat there silently, eyes closed, looking as if he were sleeping.

Tuesday, May 29, 1979

Today I put off my visit to the chapel so long that God finally refused to let me in. The door was locked. I stared at it and kept shaking the handle. I couldn't believe it. I was there, but I wasn't being let in. What a way to be told to clean up my act and stop putting God aside for my convenience! I must change my ways.

Thursday, May 31, 1979

This morning Father Burns discussed evil spirits or forces. He believes they are actually present and actively set up interference to keep us from our time with God, trip us up in prayer, and send us in other directions, away from our Lord. He taught me a way to remove temporarily some of these forces: begin by praising God, then ask him to control these forces that are interfering with our lives. We should be sure to follow the prayer by giving thanks. We often ask, but forget to give thanks and praise, which God deserves. Father Burns prayed over me and I had the sensation of a lifting of my heart. He said that people often feel "lighter" after this prayer. It is hard to put into words, but I did feel more free.

In the afternoon I went to the chapel to meditate, and before I knew it the time had stretched to thirty minutes. I was enjoying the sense of peace when suddenly I saw a hand reach out to me. It was John Morgan, from the diaconate training class. He smiled and knelt beside me to pray. I watched him for a minute and my heart felt warm. Here is John, giving up his time to come and visit the sick. God is truly with him. I represent the other side, living from sin to sin. Yet John and I have both been called to the diaconate, to serve. His role is to minister to the sick and show God to people by his example. Mine is to write down my cumbersome relationship with God, and do the best I can in living my life, simple as it is.

Sunday, June 3, 1979

My first year of training for the diaconate is over. We just had our last weekend.

Friday night we began with an open meeting and there was great concern about a squabble between the priests and the candidates. Some of the candidates are apparently being too aggressive and antagonizing their pastors. Some are being utilized to cut their pastor's lawns, and some of us (like me) are simply being ignored. The candidates implored Fausto to have the bishop "tell the pastors to accept us." I finally spoke. I told the group that we cannot change the pastors. All we can do is work within our own group to develop into the best possible deacons and to do whatever service we can. Even then, we may not be accepted by our pastors. But we can learn to love the unlovable, pray, and show what we are by example.

I can't believe I said all that. Neither could my colleagues, several of whom snorted and hissed when I finished. Fausto, however, said I was exactly right.

On Saturday a charming young nun, Sister Ann, talked about the sweeping changes occurring in religious education. She informed us that the days of training little Catholic parrots are coming to an end. Instead of memorizing the Baltimore Catechism (which is not bad in itself, but learning about God is more than memorizing a series of statements), the emphasis is shifting to developing a personal relationship with God and/or Jesus. Instead of receiving faith as a prepackaged gift, we begin a dynamic relationship at baptism, a relationship that must involve work and growth. (I love it!)

Sister Ann spoke of "A&P Catholics," those who show up for ashes and palms, but don't practice their faith the rest of the year. The rituals should not be central to our faith; faith should be our relationship with God and the centrality of Jesus in our own life, Sister Ann explained. Our thinking must shift away from "pie in the sky when you die," and "working your way to heaven." We need to learn to live our union with God right here and now on earth. Our concept of morality as law must move to morality as a response of love. Sister Ann received a standing ovation.

During our Sunday mass I again puzzled over the fact that the disciples fell asleep in the garden of Gethsemane while Jesus prayed. As I sat there daydreaming I thought I could have been in the garden with him, daydreaming or sleeping! We are pitifully human. We take so much for granted. We tire and become bored so easily. We fall asleep in the garden every day.

Tuesday, June 5, 1979

I don't think my will to get up early in the morning for prayer and exercise can hold out much longer. It is by far the most difficult chore imaginable, and I have only done it for two mornings! I almost laugh at myself. Yesterday I would sooner have died than pulled myself out of bed.

My morning prayers are a groggy cacophony. My eyes burn and my thoughts swirl in a sleepy haze. I keep looking at my clock, waiting for the fifteen minutes to be over.

Even though I am obviously failing at prayer, I feel early morning is the best time for it. Just starting my day with God is such a different feeling from "fitting him in during the day." It also gives him an early start with me. And I need as much of his time as I can get. I have noticed that when I start the day with God I feel like a butterfly spreading my wings as the day goes on. But I don't think I can keep it up. I am too weak.

I would like to make this morning time my gift to God, a sort of sacrifice, although it is not much when I think of all he has done for me. I am not waiting for my "future job" with God any more. Every day is part of my work—my prayer, this writing, and my life. I pray that I will have the strength to continue my morning prayer.

Monday, June 11, 1979

I am worried about Monsignor Burns. He is starting to have some problems with his health. Last week he suddenly lost vision in one eye, and his heart rate seems to fluctuate from day to day. He has started having a difficult time reading at the altar. I worry about him, yet much of my worry is from my own selfishness. I don't want him to leave me alone in my struggle. By sharing my life with him I am learning more about myself and my relationship with God. He seems less concerned than I am, though, constantly saying with a smile, "I'm doing pretty well for an old man."

Tuesday, June 12, 1979

A worthless day: I didn't pray; I didn't jog. I am becoming aware of my limitations as a man and as a physician. It depresses me.

Monday, July 2, 1979

The summer is passing quickly but not quietly with my children visiting. My boys finally arrived and they are spending great lengths of time painting and coloring and playing with the cat. Last night they caught their first fish from our new dock and were so thrilled they didn't want to stop until long after the sun had set and the mosquitos were feasting on our arms. The boys also insist now on hearing a bible story at bedtime, but I think I'm learning more than they are.

I find myself really missing Pat and the diaconate training program this summer. I'm already looking forward to its beginning again.

Thursday, July 5, 1979

One of the family-practice residents approached me rather gingerly this morning and asked if he could ask me something "personal." It turned out to be how I manage to be religious and also a doctor. He felt that being in medicine makes it hard to believe in something that isn't objective and tangible. My first response was, "Who do you suppose created medicine?" Obviously there is no answer. He asked if I would tell him about the experiences that led me to the Church. It isn't something I have felt free to discuss around the hospital but I told him.

Sin and spiritual direction

I have never been more aware of God's leading a questioning soul to me. I tried to answer as best I could but mainly I just listened to him. I knew that he was starting a search and that God had placed me squarely in his path. I was cautiously enthusiastic. I sensed that he did not want to be preached at and I can't stand that either. I said I'd be happy to talk more with him if he liked.

Monday, July 9, 1979

On Saturday afternoon I was sitting in the sun enjoying the peace of the moment with the sound of the wind in the pines and the water lapping at the shore. I began to meditate about the family-practice resident who had approached me on Thursday, and all of a sudden I started to tingle all over as the thought formed that I might be helpful to him. I felt I should suggest that he enter the chapel for fifteen minutes each day for a week and then discuss the individual days with me. He should try to enter the chapel with an open mind, not expecting anything spectacular. He should rather expect to feel absurd, and also to be tempted to get up and leave. Despite confusion and uncertainty, he should make himself stay. At the end of the week he will know something about spiritual life: it's beautiful. This is what God wants him to do, but he is perfectly free to choose.

I galloped into the house to tell Gretchen about my idea. She was taken aback and said I shouldn't tell him what to do. I explained that I was not going to tell him to do anything, simply make a suggestion. I don't really care whether he goes to the chapel or not. If he goes once and tells me I'm crazy, it won't bother me. Gretchen persisted, saying she had never heard of such a thing. I told her that now she had.

Tuesday, July 10, 1979

I gave the resident my suggestion today. He looked at me as if I were an idiot and said, "I don't really want to do that." Then he turned and walked out. I felt a bit foolish but I hope I planted a seed. I pray it will take root in time and not just wither. Perhaps I was overzealous; I hope I did not do anything to drive him away. Maybe I should leave spiritual direction to Monsignor Burns.

Chapter 13

A physician prays for healing

From God the doctor has his wisdom.... There are times that give him an advantage, and he too beseeches God that his diagnosis may be correct and his treatment bring about a cure.   Sirach 38:2, 13-14

Friday, July 13, 1979

Last night I prayed for the gift of healing for the first time—for Gretchen. She came home Wednesday after having a circlage for an incompetent cervix and was doing well until yesterday when she started complaining about pain in the back of her calf. It hurt her to walk and she had a small spot of cherry red inflammation showing. When I squeezed the muscle, she winced. I was afraid she had a phlebitis, possibly from her last two days of being in bed. The phlebitis didn't worry me so much as knowing it could turn into a pulmonary embolus, especially if it was deep.

Gretchen thought I was being a nervous husband. I agreed but called her obstetrician anyway. He recommended we put her leg on a heating pad and keep it elevated with a stocking on it. He also told her to take aspirin and said he would check her in the morning.

After she was all propped up I offered to pray for the leg to heal. Gretchen invited me to do so. At first I felt a bit awkward, but from reading about healing I had some idea of what to expect. I removed the heating pads surrounding her leg and placed my hands underneath. For a few minutes I was silent, trying to open myself to what I should pray for. Then I started to speak freely, with praise for Jesus and thanks for giving us the gift of healing. I asked him to bind the inflammation to himself and take away the pain. We both experienced a strange sensation then. I felt that Gretchen's leg was rippling, and she thought my fingers were tingling. I continued to sit in silence, thinking of my love for her, aware of the soft rippling against my fingers. Then I thanked Jesus for hearing our prayer.

When it was over Gretchen's leg didn't seem to be any different but we both felt better. I was more relaxed and less worried and we agreed that the prayer certainly couldn't have hurt. We started thinking that we should pray together more often. Inwardly I was glad that I had had the courage to pray openly and ask for help.

Gretchen called me about an hour ago and said she felt much better this morning. Her leg doesn't seem to be hurting the way it did when she was walking last night. I told her to stay in bed until she sees her doctor. (God uses doctors too.)

Thursday, July 19, 1979

Gretchen's leg improved slowly over the next two days. Her doctor almost admitted her but decided to wait over the weekend. Now she is fine. Neither of us is sure what effect the prayer had but we are glad we did it.

I finally got a letter from Pat, who is now in the process of converting the naval base in Cuba. He must be having some problems, though, because his letter said, "My God, my God, why have you forsaken me?"

Monday, July 23, 1979

Ever since Terry Wilson came into my office nearly a year ago I have felt linked with him in a strange way. It is as though I knew he was going to be back to see me. Today he returned for re-evaluation.

There is no sign of a recurrent tumor and a few hairs are beginning to grow back on his bald head. I have had the urge to pray with him and his wife but I haven't known how to approach the subject. I thought I would sound like a fool, and I felt that it would be awkward for me as a physician to reach out with prayer. Terry and his wife helped me without knowing it.

They handed me a brochure on cures by diet and vitamins and I told them I didn't think much of that idea because there is no evidence that vitamins or enzymes change anything with brain tumors (or any kind of tumor). Then I started fumbling for words. Terry said, "It sounds as though you have another idea." I began to explain my role in the Church as a candidate to the diaconate and my recent readings about healing prayer. I suggested that we begin to pray for Terry. He and his wife both looked shocked. I thought for a second they would walk out. He turned to his wife and said, "This is the answer to our prayer." As it turned out they were completely in favor of the idea. I told them I would call Bob, a friend in my training program who has a healing team, and see if they could come to help.

I can't believe I have opened my big mouth again. Well, God, here we go again.

Thursday, August 2, 1979

A few days ago Terry called me at home. He and his wife were having reservations about getting together to pray for healing, afraid it might be sacrilegious. I thought it would be a good idea to get together first to talk some more about it.

Last night Gretchen and I had dinner with Terry and Lynn. The evening brought forth a marvelous flow of feelings, concerns, anxieties, and faith—an absolute fountain of faith. We are reluctant and unsure. We all admitted that this new step is something we find difficult to speak about, but while talking together we feel like shouting it to the whole world. I prayed silently with thanks that I had been given a role to play in the lives of such a lovely couple. Gretchen was extremely moved and seemed to be a source of practical support for all of us. (Neither of us can believe we are actually doing this.)

Terry is now completely in favor of proceeding, and so am I. We plan to meet tomorrow night to begin our prayers. Terry has no physical signs or symptoms at the moment but I will follow him closely with clinical exams, EEGs, and CT head scans. I was very honest with him. I don't have any idea what will happen, but I know we will be heard. For some reason we have all been brought together. May God help us.

Saturday, August 4, 1979

Gretchen and I arrived on Friday evening to find Lynn pacing nervously about the living room, and Terry soaking in a tub of hot water to relieve a severe stomach pain that had just come up. We were all nervous, not knowing what to expect. Lynn said that she felt "the devil is trying to interfere." This statement surprised me. But I also grew uneasy because of a sensation I had experienced while driving to their house, one I had tried to ignore. We had passed a small house with a woman standing outside beside a car. The woman's face bothered me—I thought of the devil, or evil forces, whatever you want to call them, and I was put on my guard. It was as if I expected trouble. I thought my imagination was running away with me until we actually started our prayers.

Bob arrived with his prayer group, consisting of his wife and two other women. I could feel that they were "right" for this meeting as they came into the room. Some small talk to allay anxiety followed and then Terry began squirming in his chair, anxious to get started.

Everyone knelt down and placed their hands on Terry while I stood and placed my hands on his head. The prayer was quiet—no shouting, no flashes of light, no angels. In fact, nothing. I became aware of a force trying to block us and asked the Lord to protect us all and bind the evil to himself so we could proceed. At that point Bob stopped and took his hands away. We had prayed for about ten minutes.

Bob told Lynn to pray daily for Terry. When he said this we all felt that we needed to pray for her and began to do so. Then Terry became weak and broke away from the group; I moved over to be with him. As he sat down, Lynn suddenly collapsed to the floor. I heard the others exclaim, "Praise the Lord!" Bob explained that sometimes this happens—Lynn would be fine. "The spirit has simply overpowered her," he said. She woke up laughing. She had not fainted—she wasn't pale or diaphoretic but almost euphoric.

We sat and talked for a while. One of the women had also been aware of a blocking "evil" power. We discovered that every one, except Gretchen and me, had had something come up that had almost caused them to cancel their plans to come. Curious. The general feeling was that this meeting was very important; it had taken place for a reason, though none of us knew why. We weren't even certain who might have been healed. Some thought Lynn had been the recipient. I felt perhaps the evil had been temporarily driven away. We made no further plans except to wait and see.

Gretchen and I left feeling very close to Lynn and Terry. I can easily describe my feeling for them both as love. I think Gretchen is feeling the same. We left with a renewed sense of spirituality. We also were aware, perhaps for the first time, of actual evil forces in our lives. I knew this was the crucial time to pray for Terry, because he had had some subtle changes in his left hand. I noticed at dinner this past week that he dropped a couple of things at the table. Something sinister didn't want us interfering with his decline, and something was making Lynn feel unworthy to pray. Now, with Gretchen and me and the group cheering her on, unworthy or not, she is praying again. God help them.

Monday, August 20, 1979

I can't believe two weeks have passed since I wrote last.

Last Wednesday evening we prayed for Terry again. He had called a few days prior to that, requesting our return. This time everyone was more relaxed and no one could detect the presence of evil. But Terry was struggling. He didn't feel any change from the first prayer, and in fact felt that he was not allowing himself to "let go" and allow the Lord to work with him. Some of the women told him to "trust Jesus," but it seemed easier said than done.

I found my psychiatric talent emerging. I suggested Terry was afraid of dying, and afraid the prayer was not going to work. He started to talk then about what was holding him back and questioned his faith. I reminded him of the evening we had first decided to go forth with our prayers for healing. He recalled the great spark of faith that had allowed him to take the plunge into the unknown. We began to pray again. Suddenly I was aware of the Apostles eating their last meal with Jesus and not knowing what was in store for them. The occasion was like my first communion—so uncertain. Terry probably felt like that. I expressed my feelings aloud and heard Terry softly say, "Yes." Bob saw an image of Terry and Lynn together for a long time, but he didn't know what it meant and urged caution.

When we left, Gretchen and I felt that something was moving. We didn't know what or how far it was going, whether there would be a spiritual healing or a physical one. But something had begun.

Tuesday afternoon, August 21, 1979

Before rounds I went into the hospital chapel to pray for Terry. I looked up at Jesus on the cross and felt that he would not ignore the sick. I prayed also because I did not feel like making rounds. I did not even want to be at the hospital.

After my prayer I made rounds, visiting the sick, briefly speaking with families. There were some smiles, some questions. I felt good and wondered again why I could not feel this way all the time. Why do I have such a difficult time giving of myself? I can't seem to do what is right on my own. I need help. Fundamentally, I am a crude, nasty person who likes to take short cuts and wallow in self-adulation. How easy it is to grow complacent, fat, and happy. By myself, I am nothing. I need God in my life to help raise me above these things. But after every rise, it seems I fall right back down again.

Wednesday, August 22, 1979

Today my boys came down with crusty skin lesions that turned out to be Impetigo. I arrived home early and knew what they were as soon as I saw them (and I rarely can recognize a skin lesion). I called one of my internal medicine friends who lives a few houses down from us and asked if he would drop off some medicine on his way home.

When he came by we invited him in for a few minutes. He was very impressed with the view of the water and my new boat. Then he said he envied me for what I have. I felt depressed that he envied me for these "things." True, I enjoy them, but to be envied for them? These things are God's gifts. I am fortunate, but I shouldn't be envied. There are times I would as soon live in a monastery (if I had my wife and a TV for the football games; I can't get away from worldly things either). I ended up believing the most important thing is spending time with God in prayer—so I started in again.

Saturday evening, August 25, 1979

Last night we had Terry and Lynn over for a boat ride and dinner. Later, as the sun was setting and the evening wind stirred the pines and raised little waves in the water, Terry and I sat outside and talked about our lives, and our deaths.

I shared a meditation in which I suddenly experienced the fear of dying. I could not let go of my life. I was terrified. Then I found myself giving myself to God and suddenly my life didn't matter anymore, as long as I was with him. This experience was close to what Terry had felt during our last prayer meeting when he couldn't let go. In the morning when he prays and reads scripture he feels fine and can accept his death. But as soon as he finishes prayer and starts to move about the house, peace leaves him and he feels very alone.

We never stop long enough to think about our death. It takes us by surprise, even if we don't die suddenly. We want to hold on to our flesh and our lives as we know them, even when we believe that there is something better waiting for us. I was at ease talking with Terry, but at the same time I felt uncomfortable because I was sharing feelings about the end of my own life as I know it. I also knew, as I did when I first met him, that we are somehow linked together. I will always be with him.

I suggested that we start meeting weekly to continue our talks and to pray together. He readily agreed.

A physician prays for healing

Sunday, August 26, 1979

This afternoon I took my children to the airport. I prayed that their flight would be a safe one and hugged them goodbye. I felt a hollow ache inside as they left. The summer was suddenly over. No more cereal boxes all over the breakfast table; no more tucking them into bed or looking in on them late in the evening. I really miss them.

Monday, August 27, 1979

Just one year ago I was baptized and confirmed. I am a year old today! I would love to dwell on my accomplishments over the past year but there don't seem to be any. I knew when I started this journey that it would last forever. How does a year measure against forever? I am thankful for the journey and for God's blessing, for Gretchen, Pat Fryer, and all my children and friends.

I am also glad I started praying again with a renewed intensity this past week, partly for guidance in my prayers for Terry, and partly for myself.

Wednesday, August 29, 1979

After finishing with my office patients yesterday I went to see Terry at his house. I was greeted by Mongo, his giant German Shepherd, whose husky bark almost brought the roof down. Terry and I talked for a while, about fishing, his plans to return to the university in two weeks, going on vacation, and a little about prayer and scripture. When I was about to leave I felt I had not accomplished what I had come for: to pray for him. I asked him if he felt like praying. He did. So we retired to the relative peace of a back bedroom away from the telephone, doorbell, and Mongo, who kept dropping a ball on my foot.

The prayer was beautiful. I felt at peace and so did Terry. As we asked for healing I was aware of love.

Thursday, August 30, 1979

I have periodically had a great deal of difficulty with my feelings about Jesus Christ. I have often wanted to be Jesus Christ, with great powers. I frequently feel I am competing with him instead of loving and praising him. At times I am jealous and downright angry at him. Recently in prayer I brought this situation up. I asked him how I could love him with all these mixed, neurotic feelings. I was profoundly affected by the answer: "Russ, I am Gretchen." In my heart I could not find any anger, envy, or competitive feelings about Gretchen—only love. I was also reminded of how we were brought together by Christ and married, sacramentally joining with him.

Now my concept and feelings about Christ have changed. The competitiveness and anger I harbored seem to have melted away. Right now I am aware only of my feelings of love, and of how Christ loves me, as difficult as it must be.

Perhaps during these past few weeks of prayer for the healing of others, Jesus decided to heal the physician as well.

Chapter 14

Doctor and deacon

The deacon is not defined by what he does, but by what he is.   *Rev. Fausto Stampiglia*

Friday, September 7, 1979

I am excited about the diaconate training program starting up again. We have our first Sunday together on September 9; classes begin on the eleventh and will continue every Tuesday evening, from 5:00 to 10:30. This semester we will study the New Testament and the documents of Vatican II. On Sundays we will discuss the theory and practice of the permanent diaconate, and we will have group meetings, prayer, and mass. I feel I have been lying dormant for the summer, waiting to get back.

We met with Fausto earlier this evening for an orientation. He was in good form. He is such a beautiful person. He advised us to think hard about what we are doing in our training. He warned us again that completing the formation and the courses would not assure us of automatic ordination. He compared being a deacon to being a general—the general doesn't sweep floors and shoot the guns; in fact he might not do much at all, but he leads the people. We have been chosen by God to be leaders and to spread his word by being like his son. Although we are sinners, we must try our best. The room was silent as he then led us in a very moving, prayerful meditation for our growth in the program. We are truly blessed to have Fausto as our director.

During the meeting the new candidates from Pensacola introduced themselves. One described himself as a "hootin'-hollerin' charismatic," much to the joy of many of our number, especially Sam "praise the Lord" Devine who is forever interrupting class with his exclamations. During our break I told Fausto that I considered myself a "hootin'-hollerin' anticharismatic." He smiled and said quietly, "Amen to that."

Tuesday, September 11, 1979

I'm too wound up to sleep right now. The training classes just started up again. Five hours in a row from 5:15 p.m. on. We were like a sagging army of coffee-drinking disciples, but we were there. Our first class is Introduction to the New Testament, and the second is Documents of Vatican II. Both teachers are exceptional.

Even though I felt wiped out when the classes were over, I loved them. I love it when we open with a prayer for guidance in our learning and give praise for our teachers and our daily life. Never have I had classes like these.

Wednesday, September 12, 1979, 5:00 p.m.

We have just had to evacuate our house. Hurricane Frederick is off the gulf coast, heading right toward us. We awoke this morning to the sound of our neighbors pounding nails into plywood boards to cover their windows. I went out and tried to anchor the boat in the boat basin. I had a terrible time; the winds were so powerful I kept drifting all over the place. Finally I got two lines tied to the dock and two anchors out.

We are at the house of a friend now and the power is flickering on and off. I have already prayed several times today for the hurricane to change course, die down, leave. It is just a hundred miles away now, unleashing thunderstorms and gusty winds. I'm glad I'm with Gretchen and among friends.

5:30 p.m.
The lights are starting to flicker. I fear that our house may be lost. I called the hospital and they told me to stay here—there is nothing to do now.
We are sitting in front of the TV, spellbound, waiting.

6:00 p.m.
The TV just went out. Landfall is expected around Mobile Bay, just a few miles from where we live. Lord, help us. Turn the storm away; protect our lives and property.

Thursday, September 13, 1979, 7:30 a.m.
I can't believe I fell asleep during the storm. I kept thinking I was going to get up in a few minutes, and now it's morning. The hurricane has passed. Trees are down everywhere and the bayou has flooded almost to the back door, but it's receding. We are eating peanut butter and hard-boiled eggs for breakfast. We don't know what has happened to our house. The radio just announced that several houses in our area are totally destroyed, and many are flood-damaged. We must go see.

10:00 a.m.
Our house is ok!! It is still standing but we can't go in. The National Guard and the police are sealing the area off until the owners are all here, to protect the damaged areas. The backyard is a shambles; our boat is sitting in it like a shipwreck and looks pretty damaged. Fences are down, pieces of roof are everywhere, along with branches, boards, pilings, gas cans, and furniture. Most of it is in a pile twenty feet from our back steps.
I have to thank God for saving us and our house. If the boat sinks when we put it back in the water, it sinks.

Friday afternoon, September 28, 1979
I'm going crazy with all this work. Monday I didn't leave the hospital until the sun went down; Tuesday I was at class until 10:30 p.m.;

Wednesday was my day in the office; Thursday I had to work all evening in the Adult Primary Care Clinic and see colds and sniffles; and today I was asked to drop everything to assist the U.S. Attorney on a litigation case against the navy.

My prayer life has disintegrated again. For the past two weeks I have been thinking I must get up to the chapel and pray. The next thing I know I'm ready to go to bed because the day is over. There is just one failure after another.

My parents came to dinner last night and out of the blue my mother asked me if Jesus was a Jew. I said he was and she bristled and started to tell me I didn't really know. I repeated that he had indeed been a Jew. I could tell by the way her nose went up that Jesus had just dropped another notch in her opinion.

At the opposite extreme is Sam "praise the Lord" Devine. At our last class I went into the bathroom to find him praising the Lord at the commode. The praise continued, unabated, right through our classes. I am beginning to feel I must say something to him about his constant interruptions in class. The instructors go about their business, ignoring him, but he is beginning to drive me crazy. I try to see his good points, and there are many, but he still bugs me.

I don't have time to say anything about the classes. They are excellent but I am so pressed for time, I can hardly review my own notes.

Monday, October 1, 1979

Pope John Paul II is here in our country. A great stir is growing in Boston and Washington where he will be visiting. There is certainly little peace for the Vicar of Christ.

Only our country can manage to start great controversies about insignificant matters. A lawsuit has even been filed in Washington contending that the pope should not speak on public property because of the separation of Church and State.

I have always believed questioning is helpful. Our Church has already suffered enough for not allowing questions. Perhaps the questions having to do with birth control, ordination of women, married priests, and the roles of ministers will all be helpful as we go on. But not to the point of forgetting our faith. Through all the controversy there is a mild spirit of excitement in the air too. Boston is swelling with Catholics now, waiting for a brief glimpse of the pope, and the opportunity to share the Mass with him.

Wednesday, October 3, 1979

Terry has had some mild changes in his left arm; his left-biceps reflex is hyperactive. Otherwise he is unchanged. The EEG again shows slowing over the right frontal area, essentially unchanged from the one in March. The CT head scan is also about the same, but there is a small area of low density at the edge of the left frontal horn that is new. It bothers me but I don't know what else to do now, except to keep praying and watching. Terry has already lived longer than half of the patients with gliomas. Another six months and he will be standing among the five per cent who survive for a year and a half. He needs a lot of prayer. I will be meeting with him every Wednesday afternoon after my clinic. We will probably call the prayer group together once a month.

I must get back to my prayers.

Thursday, October 11, 1979

I'm in between patients now. It's been a terrible day—multiple sclerosis, strokes, spinal cord problems, people with canes and heading toward wheelchairs.

My prayer life is an abomination. I scratch for a minute here or there and then the minute is consumed with daily life. I'm facing my repeat board exam in child neurology so I've been trying desperately to study in the mornings despite constant interruptions.

Yesterday Gretchen found out her circlage is slipping. The doctor doesn't know whether or not it's working right now. So we are praying that it holds together. She is due January 4 but needs to get through another month for the baby to have a chance. We pray that God will allow us to bring our child into the world.

Saturday, October 13, 1979

Last night Gretchen and I went to Terry's and prayed for him with the prayer group. In addition to prayer we talked about how he was doing in school, other aspects of prayer life, and again about dying. Terry is much tougher—it's as if we are dealing with a horrendous undertaking that is not impossible but difficult and draining. (If my colleagues knew I was meeting with a patient to pray with him, they would probably crucify me. And if he does get well they will say it was because of the radiation or the surgery.)

We also prayed for Gretchen last night. Everyone (including Gretchen and me) felt very positive about the prayers. I also asked the group to pray for me. I wanted some help in being open to the Lord because of my inflated ego. When they stopped praying for me I felt as if I were being held down in the chair by a pressure on my head, so they prayed some more. One of the women asked me if I was ready to receive the Holy Spirit. I said no. I couldn't believe it. Who would say no to such a question? They explained that all I have to do is ask. But something is blocking me.

Perhaps I need to have Monsignor Burns pray for me. At times I feel as if there is a demon inside of me, mocking my prayer life and others who pray. Gretchen told me she has had feelings that I could be very important in helping Terry. But is it myself? Or is it the Spirit? Or is it the Spirit within me?

Just before we arrived Terry had a seizure, a deflating way to start. But then I have felt for a long time that things are going to get worse before they get better.

Sunday, October 21, 1979

One of the highlights of my week now is to meet with Terry. We talk about many things but mainly religion and prayer, and then we close with a prayer.

Thursday, October 25, 1979

Next Tuesday I take the boards again. I am more interested in studying this time and feel that I'm learning. I also am growing aware that I have become a doctor for some good reason. If God had wanted me to be a priest he would have guided me in that direction. But he didn't. Instead, I am to be a doctor and a deacon.

Sometimes this choice is a source of conflict for me. I want time to read about God, to go to church, to pray and study, but medicine and patients are always getting in my way.

I am aware that this "burden" of medicine I carry around as I search for God actually contains God. God isn't "out there" waiting for me to find him in books—he is right here. How can I go into church and praise God and look holy wearing my white alb and yet say, "Damn, another patient is calling me because of a headache"? There are times when I wonder if Jesus as a human didn't say the same thing once in a while. I doubt it.

Whether or not I become a deacon, I will still retain my identity as a physician. At times when I totally immerse myself in medicine I love it. At other times, though, when I want to be with Gretchen, or alone to pray, I hate to hear my beeper or the telephone. I am not like Jesus then because I growl and throw things.

Sometimes I feel that God is all around us but we don't know it. We are like babies in the womb whose mothers are all around them and they don't know it. With our present senses we can't go any farther, but at the same time we can gain an awareness of God's presence around us and within us.

Friday evening, November 2, 1979

I'm back from taking the boards again. I feel as if they took me. I have never answered "I don't know" so many times. I don't even want to think about how I did. Somehow I have to push myself now to study for my midterm exams on Vatican II and the New Testament.

Saturday, November 3, 1979

My cousin came to visit for a few days. While he was here he questioned me almost daily about my faith. He is not a member of a church, but he is searching and is probably not so far from God as I have been most of my life. I told him how I try to live my faith and he appreciated that I did not become defensive.

We must be allowed to ask questions. In this way we open ourselves to being questioned, thus showing our strength. If we have to be defensive or rigid about faith, something is wrong. We need to be open in order to grow.

Friday night we went to see the premiere showing of *Jesus*. The reviews were glowing and I expected to see great lines in front of the theater, but we walked right in. Only half the seats were filled. Where are the people who line the streets to see *Jaws*, *Apocalypse Now*, and *10*, I wondered.

In reality, the movie was not the best. It followed Luke's Gospel accurately but was dry and the acting was poor. A great deal of attention was devoted to dusty streets and toothless masses, but very little to a Jesus who had a British accent and laughed inappropriately. The tender moments came when he was with the children. I think the best current portrayal of Jesus is by Robert Powell in *Jesus of Nazareth*. There is the Lamb of God.

Sunday evening, November 4, 1979

Tonight we had a pot-luck get-together of the diaconate candidates from our parish, our pastor, and Monsignor Burns. I don't think Sam Devine and I are going to get along. He is fixated at "all you need is Jesus," and has become retarded in his growth. He doesn't read or study at all. He should not be with us.

Wednesday, November 7, 1979

Last night I got into a fight with Sam. Our class was just starting and everyone was nervous about the mid-term exam when Sam sauntered into the class with two of his "disciples." Several of us started to growl and grumble about the fact that he brings in guests who have neither registered nor paid for the courses. I decided I had had enough. It was time to confront him directly.

As our voices began to rise, a rather awesome silence grew in the room. I told Sam that bringing guests every week was inappropriate. He said I was "out of line, unchristian, and uncharitable," and mumbled something under his breath about Satan. He told his friends they might as well go home and then stormed out of the class. A sister who is taking the class came up to me and said, "I understand how you feel; I had to pay a fee. I hope this incident doesn't upset you for the test." In reality I was so upset I was shaking.

Then Father Todd entered the class with a smirk on his face, followed by Sam and his disciples. He announced loudly, "If there are problems in the class I urge you to come to me and not take it upon yourself to solve them. Remember, the main message I want you to get out of this class is that of love." Well, I felt like sinking to the floor under my desk.

The exam was passed out and I can't even remember reading the first ten questions. After fifteen minutes Father Todd called out, "Put your tests aside." We all looked around as if we didn't know what was going on and he started lecturing, telling us we could have the first five minutes of the break to finish the exam. I had been struggling with my thoughts on an essay question about the "holiness of the Church" when I pulled out my class outlines and found myself staring at the one on the holiness of the Church. At that point I felt totally unholy, and was tempted to sift through my notes and find out everything I didn't know. I resisted the temptation but I still felt like a cheat.

After the exam I apologized to Sam's two guests, not for my feelings but for my timing. I should have taken Sam aside or discussed matters with him later. Next I talked with Father Todd who was all smiles. I told him how my feelings had been building up for quite some time and that I was sick of the amens from the back of the room and the unpaid and uninvited guests. Father Todd replied that he had already discussed the matter with the bishop who thought it was a tribute to our program that guests came.

I talked with Sam next, telling him his behavior had really irritated me and my feelings had been bulding up. I started to feel better; he was grateful that I had approached him directly about it. Then he told me he loved me and was terribly bothered that he had become angry with me. "It wasn't Christian." I tried to tell him anger is human, but he didn't see it.

This morning I confessed to Father Burns. I was upset about looking at my outline during the exam. When he heard about my temptation to look over my notes as well, he laughed. He absolved me from what he called "an imperfection" with no maliciousness in it. He also said God would handle the amens in the classroom.

I feel I must write the bishop about my feelings. This training program is becoming a joke and I think he should know. I'm sure it will probably lead to another lecture on how unloving I am, but I'm going to do it anyway. The letter is coming out of love; I love the program and want it to be successful.

Saturday, November 10, 1979

I just wrote the following letter to the bishop and to Fausto (it will probably get me put out of the program):

Dear Bishop Gracida:

I am writing to you only after a great deal of thought, meditation, and prayer. What I have to say is difficult, but very important.

Our diaconate training program has some serious problems. We are receiving some rather perplexing double messages. We are told we must take a certain number of classes (or at least audit them), miss no more than three, and pass them in order to satisfy the academic requirements for becoming a deacon. Most of us have taken this to heart and are working very hard. Yet some come to class when they choose, sit in the back of the room without taking notes, shout "praise the Lord" over and over again, and bring guests who have neither paid the fees nor registered. While the majority of us are taking tests, some drink coffee outside the room, saying, "All I need is Jesus," and speaking of the ministries they are planning after ordination.

I have been through many years of professional classes and training where the expectations have always been high. If someone was unable or unwilling to satisfy the requirements he or she was placed on probation and/or expelled. I have never seen people who are not performing allowed to continue as they are in our program. It seems that training for ministry should have at least the same high standards as any college level or professional course.

I recently overheard one of our teachers say to a diaconate candidate auditor, "If you are in the class I must submit some type of grade or evaluation for you. Please see me sometime so we can talk about it." The situation brings to mind a story of four physicians aspiring to become neurosurgeons. Three are told by their department chairperson that they will learn their skills over four years by doing surgery. Then the fourth is told he must also complete the four years, but is excused from having to work in the operating room. How would you like this last one to operate on your brain? How do you think the other aspirants would feel about their training program? This is the type of double standard that exists in our program. Most of the candidates are working hard, learning, and growing. But some are not working, learning, or growing. How will these men teach sound Catholic doctrine? How are the rest of us to keep faith in our program? We are sorely lacking in guidance and discipline.

We are told on one occasion that we can expect to be ordained, and on another that some will definitely not be ordained. Just what are we supposed to expect? I find myself seriously wondering what you and the diocese want in a deacon.

In writing this letter I am reminded of my years in psychiatry dealing with groups of psychotic patients. If one or more of them started pointing at another patient, saying, "He doesn't belong with us," it was important to listen, because they were usually right. I am asking you now to hear me. Some of us should not be in the diaconate program. One thing is certain: if the "bad apples" are kept, they have a way of rotting the entire barrel. If some of our men are ordained after not lifting a finger to learn, and set free to go about the countryside teaching unsound doctrine, then I don't believe in my conscience I can be a deacon.

You may feel that I am not being loving or charitable. I am. I am writing this letter because I love the program and see a great need for this type of ministry. But I also see the need for quality and not quantity. If some candidates must be asked to leave, I do not see this as uncharitable or unloving, but exactly the opposite. Those who are not suitable to be ordained ministers can still serve useful functions in the Church and work to build up the body of Christ. Stringing them along may well deprive them of another doorway leading to a more gratifying purpose in their own lives, and for God.

I realize the program is new in the diocese and problems are to be expected. I am amazed at times to think of the many positive strides that we have all made. I wanted you to know about some of the problems "here in the trenches" though, because they concern me and many of us in the class.

I thank you sincerely for your consideration of my thoughts.

Monday, November 12, 1979

We had an excellent weekend retreat as part of our diaconate studies. Father Rimes was our director while Fausto was off in Rome, defending his doctorate. Rimes was superb. He is a Jesuit from Springhill College in Mobile where he is rector. He talked about the humanness of Christ and how we work so hard to try to make him something other than human. The temptations are either to ignore his human side and see him as "mainly God," or to see him as just the opposite, merely a "good man." The class got into a stir when he told us that Jesus didn't know he was the Christ when he was an infant. He had to grow and learn his Father's will, just as we do. We have to let Jesus be human—he was. We also have to allow God to be God; he isn't loving today and wrathful tomorrow.

Father Rimes reminded me of Pat. I miss him. I wonder how he is.

Thursday, November 15, 1979

Gretchen started to bleed yesterday. We were afraid she was beginning to dilate prematurely. We happened to be with Terry and Lynn at the time and as we set off to the hospital they said some prayers that everything would be all right. It was. A stitch had caused some bleeding. Were we relieved! It was a curious experience to have Terry and Lynn pray for us after we have been praying for them. We were glad to have their prayers.

Friday, November 23, 1979

I passed my boards! I'm finally board certified in both psychiatry and neurology. I guess persistence pays off.

Chapter 15

Questions

Monday, December 3, 1979

I met with Father Burns on Saturday and we talked about my drifting away from prayer and meditation. It seems I am always trying to begin again. It is so easy to slip away from spending time with the Lord.

I am far away, wrapped in my cloak of humanness and busy, ant-like activities. Why is it such a struggle to grow in the spiritual life? Why did God make us like this—always obsessed with our little lives? Where is he? How do I find my way back again?

It was so easy at first. Prayer was exciting, stimulating. Pat guided me and helped me. Now look at me. I have turned into a Sunday Catholic. What is even worse, I wear an alb and stand at the altar. I flounder; I stumble; I am swollen with pride and I am always trying to find you, God. You know that, don't you? Yet all you ever do is tell me to write. Imagine! You want me to write this nonsense. For what purpose?

I must find a way to get going again. I have a book of daily meditations I might use. Maybe I should begin recording my prayer times on a calendar; then I will be able to catch myself slipping away. Help me, Lord.

Sunday, December 9, 1979

Yesterday was our diaconate formation day. (Since changing to formal classes we don't have an entire weekend.) I opened the day with a presentation I have developed on the shroud of Turin. I think it went well and I enjoyed doing it.

After my talk, Fausto gave a lecture on the role of the priest in the Old and New Testaments. He made the point that priests were always considered "professionals," and that they should indeed be professional. He emphasized the work that is necessary to be a cleric: "You cannot be like a doctor who gets by on his reputation in the hospital as a great lover of the nurses, someone who might be a great lover but a lousy doctor." He looked at me then—great timing. The translation of this was, "You can't get by in ministry on your own charismatic feelings and your own thoughts about scripture." It reminds me of something I once wrote.

Father Rimes offered mass and made it a touching affair. The liturgy has to be the most beautiful part of our Church. It is timeless and priceless.

After a community lunch Gretchen and I left early because her legs were swelling and I needed a "sanity" break. Since getting my board results I have had to catch up with the hospital and lecture schedule. Gretchen felt she could not make it through the entire day. She looks larger every day now as her delivery date approaches. Maybe we'll have a Christmas baby.

I have said this so often yet I never tire of saying it: I surely love Gretchen.

Monday, December 10, 1979

I have prayed daily now for the past week. This time I am using some props. I have a small book on daily prayer that I carry in my overloaded briefcase and put in a conspicuous place as a reminder. I have been making myself pray and meditate for a minimum of fifteen minutes. I usually start by reading scripture or a meditation and then try to place myself in an open frame of mind. I think it has gone fairly well, for a change.

My daily prayers are a bit different from when I first started. The struggle is still present. It continues to take an enormous effort to pray, but the book has helped tremendously. Almost always the first five minutes of prayer are a struggle just to get into it, so I think spending at least fifteen minutes is important.

I am not expecting so much from prayer any more. Even though I want a dialogue, I don't look for it. In some ways I don't anticipate much at all. When I can manage to scrape together only fifteen minutes a day for God, why should I expect anything from him? I still feel that he is there, waiting patiently for me to mess things up again.

Thursday, December 13, 1979

I feel that prayer is sustaining Terry. I wish I could be more concrete about it, but all I have to go on are my feelings. I also know that only ten percent of patients with this type of brain tumor have lived this long.

Tuesday, December 18, 1979

I have been successful in praying and meditating daily for three weeks now. Weekends seem exceptionally difficult. It is curious that I have more trouble disciplining myself on holidays and weekends than I do in the middle of a busy day. Father Burns believes we have the most difficulty praying on holidays or when we are sick.

Gretchen and I sat together last night for about an hour and talked about spiritual life. We don't "just sit together" that often any more with all we do (writing, medicine, diaconate studies, ceramics, housecleaning, and so on), so it was an enjoyable time. She admitted she is afraid of God's pulling the rug out from under her feet, especially in her relationship with me. I have the same fear but I tend to look at it as part of life rather than God's doing.

I started reflecting on my daily prayer at that point. It seems clear to me that this must be done in order to prepare and sustain myself in a spiritual life. One obvious reason is that if I get to know God on a daily basis, very often by his seeming absence, I am not so disappointed when the inevitable crisis occurs and I turn to him and don't get any apparent answer. Our human way is to ignore him until our roof caves in and then pray that he replace the roof. When he doesn't seem to hear us then we start shouting about his being on vacation and never listening. Like any relationship it be must worked at. And as in any relationship it is easy to grow complacent, just as Gretchen and I have periodically done. This is exactly the time we most need to stop and talk to each other.

Saturday evening, December 29, 1979

I made a blunder tonight while I was doing a reading at mass. I said "alleluia" and everyone stood. In a loud voice I continued, "The Spirit of the Lord is upon me—oh, oh—maybe it isn't; I'm on the wrong page." After mass Father Burns cocked his head at me and said, "You see how the Spirit gives us the words."

Gretchen is having a few contractions—I'd better go.

Friday, January 4, 1980

A new year and a new baby! On the morning of January 2 Christine Mary Packard, seven pounds, four ounces, was born. Gretchen's labor was only four hours long and everything went well. Mother and daughter are rooming-in and enjoying each other's company. It's a delightful experience.

Friday, January 18, 1980

I think the Lord has blessed us with a night owl! Christine wants to sleep all day and bellow all night.

Classes have started up again. We have the fiery Father Todd teaching us sacramental theology and a parish priest lecturing about the Gospel of John. So far I don't like either of the classes. Father Todd is going over Thomas Aquinas word by painful word and I don't know if I'm learning anything. Our other instructor is turning the most interesting gospel into the most boring. As the five hours of classes dragged by this week I found myself squirming.

Terry is stable. I pray with him once a week. I don't know what's happening. One week I find hyperreflexia in an arm where I haven't seen it before; the next week it's gone. I find myself wondering if I really saw it. He feels that God is with us when we pray. I guess I do too. He surely doesn't sail in on the back of a dove. I feel that it is important to keep praying, but at times I wonder why.

I'm feeling almost the same way about my daily prayers and meditation. Maybe I'm just getting good at sitting still for fifteen minutes and calling it "God's time." Some days I daydream and wait for it to end. I don't understand this spiritual life at all. Then because I don't understand I start getting mad and I want to throw up my hands and walk away. But that big creep in the sky won't let me.

Monday, January 21, 1980

Every time I write I feel other eyes are reading my words. A curious feeling.

I'm in a slump now. For the first time since I was baptized, I am feeling a sense of apathy about what I am doing. My questioning is nothing new; it's the attitude of "why bother?"

I have not enjoyed my diaconate classes lately. I don't look forward to Tuesday nights. They are more like a burden. I find myself wondering if I really want to be a deacon.

Fausto came up to me last week and told me that he and the bishop are interested in my joining the permanent diaconate board as the "psychiatric advisor" when I am ordained. The idea turns me off. I left psychiatry because I didn't like doing it (even though I admit that psychiatry is where my innate talents lie). I don't want to become a deacon to be a psychiatrist again. Why go through the whole process if that is what they want? Why do I have to be a deacon to use a talent I already have?

Gretchen asked me last week what I would like to do as a deacon. I didn't know. I think I would enjoy preaching at mass once in a while.

If that's all I want to do, why should I go on?

I'm not even sure what Church means any more. I feel flat.

Where is God anyway? I think that absence is what I am most tired of. I don't feel a personal relationship with Jesus or God or the Holy Spirit. Do they care? I don't feel them talking to me. Does God really make life any better?

Friday, January 25, 1980

Spiritual life is such a frustration. Why can't I be simple-minded? I am not just struggling through the desert; I've run right into a cactus patch. Everywhere I look in the Bible someone is talking to God or he is talking to someone. I talk to a vacuum and hear nothing. Why? What am I missing?

I feel somehow the answer rests in Jesus. To see the truth I must look at Jesus. Ever since we humans began to think about God we have been trying to define just who and what he is, but our puny minds get no nearer to a definition. Few of us can grasp abstract ideas, but even a simple mind can grasp a picture. Jesus is that picture. We can look at him and say, "That is what God is like." Jesus did not come to talk to humans about God; he came to show us what God is like, so the simplest mind might know him as intimately as that of the greatest philosopher.

I have just written my answer, so why must I learn this over and over? I don't have a simple mind. That is part of my problem. I'm too much into a head trip. I have abandoned my heart for my mind. Love must make the difference. Love must be the great interpreter. Somewhere in William Barclay's writing I read that love can grasp the truth when the intellect is groping and uncertain. Love can realize the meaning of something when research is blind. Obviously we can never understand Jesus, nor help others understand him, unless we take our hearts to him as well as our minds.

I have had much "inner encouragement" to write these thoughts despite my own discouragement. I hope through my pride, arrogance, and stupidity I can understand what I have written.

Monday, February 11, 1980

I'm still in the depths. Last week I got the flu and missed two days of work. I hate being the only neurologist here. If I miss a day or two, everything sits and waits for me. The pace has been maddening. My appointment schedule is backed up into the middle of March and everyone is clamoring at my door because of the long wait. In my Christian way I told them all to stuff it.

Wednesday, February 13, 1980

I think the only thing I do well is sin. I should have been a pharisee. The more I look at the Bible the less I understand. God left us a two-thousand-year-old book that nobody understands. We just argue about it. Then someone refuses medical care and five of his children die because "it's clearly written in the Bible."

The only good thing about being sick last week was that I missed my diaconate classes. A friend took notes for me. I can follow the notes on sacramental theology fairly well but the ones on the Gospel of John are a nightmare. For four weeks the teacher has been obsessed with what year the damn thing was written and how many authors wrote it and who disagrees with whom.

There must be something good that's happened.

Christine is a delight. She is our sunshine on these bleak winter days. Sometimes I think when I am ranting and raving about God's not being around, he is right under my nose. I yell and scream and shake my fist at God and all the while he is smiling at me from the eyes of a babe!

Friday, February 29, 1980

Sam Devine has been dropped from the diaconate program. He had a meeting with the bishop and never came back to class. Rumors are rampant but no one knows what really happened.

Our first class of candidates, who are one year ahead of me in the program, will be ordained in May and it isn't clear yet how many that will include. For various reasons a couple of the men have requested that they not be ordained just yet. Some who expected to be "automatic" choices have been delayed the longest and have been asked to reappear before the bishop in another month. Actually I'm pleased that the selection process is being taken seriously.

I recently mailed a letter to my ex-wife after praying that she be rid of the bitterness that fills her. (I also prayed for myself that I be healed of my own bitterness which I so like to deny.) I invited any or all of my children to come for Easter vacation. I was nice. I didn't threaten but made the offer an invitation. No response. I wrote again enclosing a self-addressed stamped envelope. No response. What else is there to do?

Last week when Terry and I were praying together he called me "a hotline to God." I didn't tell him that most of the time I feel disconnected. At times I do feel I have a gift for "holding back storms" (I've never quite understood this myself), and I am wondering if his tumor is not a symbolic storm. It does seem to be calm at the moment.

Thursday, March 6, 1980

I finally heard from my ex-wife. She asked for more money. There wasn't even a reference to having the kids come for Easter. It seems that all I do is lay myself open to get stepped on.

Last Sunday Christine was baptized at mass. She was perfectly delightful, squirming a bit and wrinkling her forehead at the water. She didn't cry, but I almost did. The baptism was really a welcome into the community. The CCD class had made cards for her and the wives had baked cookies and cakes to have with coffee after the mass. Pat Fryer was the godfather but a friend stood in for him. This is the way baptism should be: the parents taking an active part in the child's spiritual life and the entire community involved also, a plunge into the life of Christ.

I think I am beginning to enjoy my diaconate classes again. The Gospel of John has become much more interesting and sacramental theology is meaningful too. We have another retreat coming up this weekend. I'm looking forward to it after missing the last two because of travel and the flu.

Wednesday afternoon, March 19, 1980

Today Monsignor Burns and I talked about my writing. I have been discouraged about my failure to find a publisher for my first book, *The Pysch Wards*. I have accumulated enough rejection slips to paper my walls. The universities say it is "too commercial." The commercial publishers say it is "not commercial enough and too personal." Father Burns and I talked about the Lord's role in my book. If he wants it published he will find a way. Perhaps it has another purpose, for another day.

Meanwhile, Father Burns suggested that I pray the Psalms. He suggested that I go through them until I find one that appeals to me and then meditate on it. I haven't done much yet with the Psalms. Perhaps there are some appropriate for struggling writers.

Monday, March 24, 1980

Monsignor Burns died last night. He became ill Friday evening while leading the people in stations of the cross. One of the women hurried him to the hospital as he struggled to catch his breath. He had severe congestive heart failure and nearly died the first night.

I saw him yesterday. He looked pale, fragile, and weak. His lips and nail beds were a dusky blue color and he spoke in a breathless, tired voice. Every now and then he coughed up some blood-tinged sputum, exhausting himself even further. His mind was clear, though, and he said he was ready to die. I cried and held his hand, thanking him and our Lord for allowing us our weeks together. I told him I loved him and would carry with me for the rest of my life the lessons I have learned from him. He thanked me. At one point his face contorted in pain and then he smiled weakly, saying he hated his urinary catheter.

I'm crying again now, as I write.

God, I'm sorry to lose him. He has meant so much to me, and to our community. I've loved him and now I ache with his loss. I am so thankful, though, that I was able to spend those last few minutes with him. Such a grand old man.

As I turned to leave him, I suddenly had the urge to pray with him. He had always been the one to pray for us. This time *I* prayed. As I thanked the Lord for hearing my prayer and gave him praise, I realized that the man I was praying with had taught me how to pray. When I finished, he took my hand and squeezed it, thanking me. God rest his soul.

Wednesday, March 26, 1980

Last night Gretchen and I went to the wake for Monsignor Burns. He looked peaceful, resting in his casket. Rosary beads were intertwined in his fingers, but he was pale and his face was puffy. I stared for a few minutes and then went back to the pew. I choked through the rosary, my tears falling on the beads.

The funeral mass is tonight. I couldn't face it. There are to be a hundred priests there as well as the bishop. I feel that I said goodbye that last day in the hospital. I'm glad I had that. It was a personal goodbye that I needed badly.

I guess I should think of the spirit of Leo Burns. His body is lifeless now, but his spirit is where it has striven to be for an entire lifetime. I wouldn't be surprised if he is leading a retreat for the Holy Trinity.

Meanwhile, the student must pull himself together and go on with his journey. After the rosary I met Father Todd on the steps and told him Monsignor Burns had been my teacher. He said, "Now you need another teacher." (Helpful as always.) But where do I begin? Perhaps I should say, where do we go from here, Lord?

Monday, April 14, 1980

It's been two weeks since Father Burns died. I don't feel too bad now. I miss him but I think he was ready. Yet now Wednesday mornings have an empty feeling.

My diaconate classes are almost over. The finals are next week. My next goal is to go fishing and get away from everything. Between writing, studying, and making rounds I feel as if I haven't had a weekend off in ten years.

I seem to be rambling. This is supposed to be my time for spiritual thoughts. I continue to feel that my praise and thanks to God are often empty. I'm not sure I mean them. Yet I am in God's presence. Why?

Chapter 16

A new beginning: on retreat

Thursday, April 24, 1980

It seems as though I haven't written in ages. I don't know what to write about. The days are passing quietly. Many of my major life events are over and I'm waiting for a new set to begin. I am not in the midst of writing any papers; my board exams are over; the diaconate training program is over for the summer; and I'm waiting for my service obligation with the navy to end.

At our last diaconate weekend of the year I talked with Father Rimes about his taking over as my spiritual director. He is extremely busy at Springhill College and nearly said he did not have the time, but he invited me to come over and said we would try it. I'm going to combine the visit with a mini retreat. I will go Monday evening for dinner at the rectory and stay there until Wednesday morning, just to meditate and pray under his supervision. I'm looking forward to it.

Monday evening, May 5, 1980

I'm so excited I can barely think, much less write in any sensible way. I have been wanting to make a retreat for months and now all of a sudden I'm here, courtesy of Father Bob Rimes and the Jesuit residence at Springhill College.

I left behind a busy day of patients to arrive around 5:30 p.m. I found Springhill without difficulty but stumbled around the campus a bit until I found the residence. I entered a door that looked as if it were built for giants and heard Father Rimes's voice echoing above me. I climbed the winding old staircase and ran right into him. He met me with his usual smile and firm handshake. He has the enthusiasm of Pat Fryer. Since I arrived almost at the dinner hour my tour was short but I did get my bags and my typewriter tucked away in my room.

The room is like a cheap motel room: light blue flaking paint on the walls, a soft flabby bed, wooden chair, table, and kneeler. There is also an old desk lamp with a shade that was left by the Confederate Army and a plain sink with a dirty glass. A single large window opens onto a courtyard and a view of the back of the chapel. There are no curtains; a steam pipe rises out of the floor and runs through a hole in the ceiling. I'm excited to be here. God lives in places like this.

The rest of the rectory is much like my room. The decorator must have been the same one who designed sleeping quarters for interns and residents. Spartan, also rather dark. The place could be very gloomy in winter. But right now I am delighted.

The dining area contained several round tables, each with a tureen of hot soup. Father Rimes introduced me to approximately twenty bearded, bespectacled, serious-looking occupants. No one wore a collar. I was feeling nervous as we started to eat. I didn't know what to say or how to handle myself around these scholarly religious men. Finally, a gruff bull of a man with twinkling friendly eyes (who turned out to be the president of the college) exclaimed something about "bullshit." Suddenly I felt right at home. The conversation shifted from the pope and his stand on politics to the Iranian crisis, then turned to involve the stranger in their midst, me. Our dinner of lamb chops continued over the topics of deacons, neurologists, and multiple sclerosis.

After dinner Father Rimes and I talked for an hour about what I want to do here. I mumbled and stammered and ended by saying I wasn't exactly sure. I was just very pleased to be here. I had expected to be on my own because Father Rimes had warned me

A new beginning: on retreat

that he would probably be very busy. But he is quite free and I ended up unexpectedly speechless. We decided to meet two or three times during my stay. I told him that I have come here to take time out to ponder my relationship with God. He said he will try to listen and help facilitate this relationship. I believe he has more spiritual insight than I could absorb in a lifetime.

Now that I'm in my room I think I will stop writing and pray a bit.

Twenty minutes later

I'm having trouble getting into prayer. I should have known: I always have trouble with change. I know what is going to happen: by Wednesday morning I'll be finally ready to start and it will be time to go back and see patients again. Perhaps I should begin where Father Rimes suggested: "Just praise God for allowing us to be here to share this time together."

Twenty minutes later

I probably should be praising the Lord and praying my head off now instead of writing. But I'm writing a living memory, and perhaps one day it will enable others to take a few minutes or a few days out of the daily stream of life to strengthen their relationship with God.

God has indeed been kind to me. I'm blessed with a life that I enjoy, a wife and a new baby daughter whom I love and who together have given me the freedom to be myself and to come here. I also think of my older children and pray for them. Even my ex-wife, who is one of my crosses, I pray for.

I must call Gretchen and tell her how marvelous I feel at this place.

Tuesday morning, May 6, 1980, 7:00 a.m.

I had to put the mattress on the floor. The old set of springs made me feel as if I were sleeping in a bowl of spaghetti.

As I went to bed last night I couldn't decide how to begin my prayers. Suddenly I thought, "Why not begin at the beginning with Genesis?" So I read the first chapter. "In the beginning...."

In the beginning I was nothing. My first memory was a dream. I was just an infant then, snuggled comfortably in my crib, months away from experiencing even simple dreams. Suddenly, out of the darkness of my childhood slumber, a woman appeared to me dressed in dazzling white like a bride. She was glowing with radiance and love, a true light in the darkness. Her presence filled me with warmth, inner peace, and life. I continued to sleep then—and thirty years passed.

At times I wonder if I was on the verge of crib death and an angel of life saved me. Or was it an image of Mary? I know it is unusual to have a dream as a first memory, from a psychiatric standpoint.

In the beginning. It seems that we are always at a new beginning and always at an end. I keep coming back to my dream. Darkness covered the abyss. Then God said, "Let there be light." A woman coming as a light in darkness. Curious.

It's almost time for breakfast now—better go.

8:30 a.m.

I've just had the largest breakfast I've had in months. I feel bloated. The conversation centered around the upcoming deacon ordinations. My companions are impressed with our quality. Later this morning Father Rimes and I are going to meet for another hour.

11:00 a.m.

Another good talk, after which we went to a small side chapel and Father Rimes said mass. It seemed very special—just the two of us. Actually I guess there were three of us!

I'm writing now out in the courtyard, basking in the sun and getting sprinkled by a drizzling fountain. I enjoyed the last hour with Bob Rimes. He sat in his rocker and we talked about many things, but the topic invariably drifted back to discernment. What is coming from God? How is Christ working in our lives? I gave him a copy of this journal to read during the summer. I'll be interested in hearing what he thinks about it.

It is really peaceful here, very much like our mass earlier today. It isn't the type of peace the world can offer; it is a different sort of peace. I hope God will allow me to come here often.

11:30 a.m.

I still find it difficult to be alone in God's presence. I want to run (literally—I feel like jogging). I am anxious, naked in his presence. There is really no place to go—no telephones, patients, TVs. I can't escape facing myself here. But why should I try to escape? I thought I wanted to face myself and my relationship with this mystery. Maybe it's because I'm faced with myself as I am, weak and wanting to be omnipotent without God's help. I'm a hopeless case. I can't see myself apart from God, and I can't see myself with him, either.

Noon

I've just read some passages from John about those who sow and those who harvest. Some of us may be given the challenge of sowing and never reaping. Many work and never see the result of their labor—but no work for Christ will fail. Sometimes I wonder about this writing. What will happen to it? Why is it important that I do this? Why not some Jesuit whose life is devoted to God? Why must I, a physician and a lowly candidate to the diaconate, be typing away into the night about all of this? Questions, Lord. Questions.

1:30 p.m.

A nice lunch with Bob Rimes. (I don't just *feel* bloated anymore; I *am* bloated.) After lunch we had another brief talk, then he decided it was time for me to be off on my own.

Back to the sunshine. I'm sure people will think I'm here for a vacation with the tan I'm getting. I guess they are right to some extent. Why not vacation with God? He gave us the sun, too, didn't he?

3:30 p.m.

I have been rereading Anthony Bloom's *Beginning to Pray*. I especially enjoy his chapter on "The Absence of God." How important it is to realize that prayer is an encounter and a relationship. I am constantly getting angry at God for "not being there." After all, I give him fifteen minutes a day. The problem is that for those fifteen minutes I am usually thinking about going fishing, being out in my boat, giving a lecture, and so on. What about the twenty-three and three-fourths hours during which God might want to knock at my door? "Sorry, God, I'm too busy." I am indeed a great deal more absent than he is. Nevertheless, I persist in blaming him for his absence.

The fact that God can make himself present or absent to us is part of this live and real relationship. How often do we want *something* from him and not *him* at all. What sort of relationship is that? Do we aim at what friendship can give us, or is it the friend or wife or husband whom we love?

7:30 p.m.

I can feel my time slipping away. I want more. Bob Rimes was out so I ate with some of the other Jesuits tonight. I enjoyed talking with them. Some of them have been teaching here for twenty to thirty-five years! A name comes up in conversation and invariably somebody at the table knows that he was in his art history class in 1962!

I'm back in my room now. There was a big thundershower just a few minutes ago. Now it's clear already. I feel a sadness welling up inside. I wish I didn't have to leave. At first I thought the Jesuits were a bit odd. They get together at dinner and talk and then quietly melt away minutes later, not to be seen again until the next meal. Every once in a while I hear the clatter of a typewriter or the flushing of a toilet somewhere, but otherwise all is quiet.

Thank you, Lord, for letting me be here even for this short time. Although I'm leaving in the morning, it's been a new beginning for me, a new day.

Wednesday, May 7, 1980

The retreat is over. I'm back in the office seeing patients again. My spirits have plunged since coming back. I'm sure a few more days at Springhill would have had me climbing the walls but I find myself wishing I were back there. At first it was as though I had received a spiritual boost to come back and face patient after patient, but it wore off in about an hour.

A cluster-headache patient has come back unchanged; another patient broke out in a rash from the medicine I gave her. Still another called me on the phone to complain about his bill: "Now let me tell you, one country boy to another...." I cut him off and told him I was not a "country boy." If he had a medical problem I would be happy to discuss it, but I could not explain why his insurance had not covered his EEG; he would have to talk to my secretary. "No, boy, you're the man I need to talk to." I finally convinced him I do not do the billing so I couldn't help him with it. "Boy, I just don't know how you can run a business letting the women do it."

My transsexual patient came in next with a "terrible headache" but was very pleased with how his chest is growing from hormone treatments he's getting from another doctor. He offered to show me but I said I could see. I gave him his medicine and he came back an hour later: "Honey, somebody broke into my car and took every bit of my medicine...." After he left, a patient called for a four-month supply of medication because she has to testify out of state at a big trial and is going to be held in a hotel all that time by the FBI. She swears her story is true. The problem is that she has called for "all the medicine" four times in the past six weeks. I told her I would not give her any more. She hung up on me.

So this morning I was praying humbly and this afternoon I'm cursing the rabble that are the "salt of the earth." The spirit life and God are there at Springhill and they are also here in the real world. But I am a long way from knowing them.

Chapter 17
Who am I?

Sunday, May 11, 1980

Yesterday the first class of permanent deacons was ordained for the diocese of Pensacola-Tallahassee in a beautiful ceremony.

I saw it first-hand, kneeling for most of the ceremony in front of the bishop and holding the sacramentary. First I was asked to be an acolyte "to carry the cups to the altar." Next, someone said, "Would you mind carrying the book?" What could I say? I carried the book. What I didn't realize was that I had to hold it open for the bishop during the entire ordination rite.

We had a very well organized master of ceremonies. The problem was that his follower didn't know when to follow. Once when I pranced up behind him he glanced over his shoulder and whispered to me to go back. He didn't need me yet. I tried to look inconspicuous in front of a thousand people and the cameras from the local TV station.

Despite all this fumbling around I had an encounter with the real spirit of Christ. I was led to the step directly in front of the bishop and asked to kneel there while holding the book open. The step was hard and almost immediately my knees began to hurt. The bishop's dark eyes carried the conviction of the words that he read. I could not listen; my knees were screaming and my back and arms were aching. My face broke out in a sweat. I was afraid I would drip onto the pages. At a break in the reading the bishop looked at me and asked in a whisper if I was all right. His concern gave me the strength to answer that I was. At least I knew then that I would not faint. I said it was hot. He asked one of the priests nearby to fetch something for me to kneel on. A purple pillow was brought and placed gingerly under my flattened knees. The relief was a true blessing.

The bishop addressed all nineteen candidates individually. I started to feel the hard surface under the pillow and great beads of sweat broke out on my forehead, face, and neck, rolling down into my alb. My shirt was clinging to me. For a moment I wondered if I would collapse, making a spectacle of myself. Then I heard the quiet words, "Would you like to stand for a moment?" Words of concern. I knew it would not be appropriate for me to stand but I looked at him again and thanked him, saying I could manage. I slid my hand through the alb and into my pocket to get a tissue to mop my brow. After I wiped my face, somehow I knew I would make it, and I did. I don't know if I could have managed without the bishop's concern. Few noticed the drama within the drama and for many I'm sure the brief noddings from bishop to acolyte went unnoticed. While the candidates came forward to receive the laying on of hands, the book of the Gospels, and a blessing, I was inches away, painfully aware of each one kneeling beside me as I prayed that time would pass quickly.

I'm sure the new deacons will remember their ordination well: the excitement, the spiritual meaning, and the personal reflections. But I will also remember being there, and with a bishop like ours I would have volunteered for two more hours if necessary.

Monday, May 12, 1980, noon

This morning I started my daily prayer and was getting nowhere again. I forced myself to read a prayer. Halfway through it my mind wandered away to preparing a lecture on coma, and from there to getting the boat out next weekend to go fishing. I became very frustrated with myself and stopped reading.

I remembered Father Rimes saying that prayer begins by putting yourself in the presence of God. Easily said, and nothing new. I have heard it over and over again. This morning I simply didn't know how to put myself in his presence.

I started repeating "the body of Christ" over and over again. I've never tried that before. No one had ever told me to try it. But while I was saying the words I could visualize handing out the sacred bread at communion. Suddenly I was reminded of the ordination. During the distribution of communion a guest deacon from Mobile dropped a piece of the consecrated bread on the floor. Gretchen noticed but no one else did. The deacon stared at it but didn't do anything and it started to be kicked around by the shuffling feet. Finally a newly ordained deacon who was giving out wine saw what was happening. He left his station, interrupted the line of people, picked up the bread that by now had been reduced to a ragged bit of crumbs and ate it.

I continued to repeat "the body of Christ," reflecting on that piece of bread. Jesus was there, being kicked about by the crowd, while one of his own ministers watched his being trampled. Blessed was the one who saw all of this and had the courage and the stomach to consume the bread.

Today, through the body of Christ, I think that I did indeed put myself in the presence of our Lord. The surprising thing is that he is always there. I'm the one who isn't. I have not been putting myself in his presence for months.

Friday, May 30, 1980

I feel discouraged. My first book continues to be rejected. At this point I have lost my drive. I have a feeling that the work is destined for the bottom drawer of my desk.

I have prayed often for it to be successful. I have even prayed that it need not be successful—as long as it is published. I suppose I am being foolish, but after five years of scratching and clawing for minutes here and there, mornings of locking myself in the office and avoiding the telephone, Saturdays writing, writing, writing—all I have are twenty some-odd rejections to show for my efforts. What are you trying to teach me, Lord? Have I reached my limit? Do you want me simply to check reflexes in my office for the remainder of my days? And what is the purpose of this current writing? Who am I, Lord, to do this? I don't understand.

I was so excited when I sent my first book off. I used to wait for the mail to come; now I go out of my way to avoid it. I guess I should be pleased that two editors wanted to read the book. That's nice. Like being told to apply for a job next year.

I'm not being very spiritual today. Just a grumbling human. But that's all I am. Lord, I need your support. Teach me how to fail with humility. If I find you through my failure, I will have success.

Tuesday, June 3, 1980

Sometimes medicine can be cruel. Yesterday evening I carried a piece of paper over to our neighbors the Carey's for the new local neighborhood phone directory. Bob was tending his yard, trimming the hedge, watering his flowers. He and his wife, Barbara, moved here this past year after he retired from the army. They are a delightful couple, taking late afternoon walks, playing tennis, enjoying the beach. I was about to leave when Bob (almost in passing) commented on his wife's breathing difficulties. Over the past four weeks it seems she has become progressively more short of breath, to the point of having to rest at intervals when walking up the stairs in their house. She sleeps propped up on pillows and is unable to play tennis anymore, or even to walk to the court down the street. Two weeks ago she saw a physician's assistant who diagnosed bronchitis and didn't take a chest x-ray. She is forty-eight and a heavy smoker. I told Bob to bring Barbara to my office in the morning and I would take a chest x-ray.

I just saw the x-ray. Barbara has a massive pleural effusion on the right lung and a moderate effusion on the left. There is also a suggestion of a mass on the right. Primary diagnosis: malignant effusion. It almost made me physically sick. She sat in my chair, speaking in broken sentences in order to breathe, eyes filled with concern. I transferred her to one of the internists who plans to admit her and tap the effusion today.

How suddenly life can change. I called Gretchen and she cried. I feel like crying. I look at Bob in the waiting room, alone with his thoughts. I could be there in his place. I pray for them both.

Sunday, June 8, 1980

I think I may stop writing. It doesn't seem to be going anywhere and my great craving is beginning to dwindle away. I have lost the drive that I used to have. I think part of my reluctance is related to my transition from the navy into private practice in September. So far I'm not even sure about that change because the navy hasn't yet acknowledged that it is letting me out.

I am discouraged about the beating my first book is taking. The experience has been a real eye-opener. The book seems to appeal only to the women who typed it for me. It has been hard to get slapped in the face week after week with rejection after rejection. I used to be able to take rejection, be almost challenged by it. The first wave of rejections stimulated me to put out more, write a better query letter, send better pages, revise, rewrite. I believed in what I was doing. Today I'm not so sure. I think maybe it's garbage. Now I'm wondering about this writing. Everything is garbage.

Obviously this journal is very personal. Many people keep a spiritual journal. Why should this one be published? How could this rambling be of use to God? He may want me to be only a doctor. And if I'm just meant to see patients then this writing is taking time away from practicing better medicine. This journal isn't a hobby I do for fun. I'd rather scuba dive or fish or spend time with Gretchen and Christine.

This page may be my last, but I have a nagging feeling that God wants me to write it and give up, quit, crawl around—and ask him for help.

Monday, August 4, 1980

Yes, it is August already. I haven't been writing. I think my writing is a big farce. A divine practical joke.

Perhaps the first part of the book had some meaning but then it became lost. Or am I the one who became lost? At any rate my first book is now in the bottom drawer. It is gone and so are all my hopes for writing.

It is very hard to open my eyes to the truth about myself. I'm a terrible writer. Well, maybe I'm not terrible; but nobody cares about what I have to say except myself. *The Psych Wards.* Hell, I should be on one.

I search for a purpose that writing has served in my life, but that spark, that pulsing inner desire that drove me for so many years is gone. I wrote every morning for three years, and every Saturday I remodeled my words to make sentences flow, become beautiful. Now the beautiful sentences are gathering dust in a bottom drawer. But the urge to write, that nagging force, has quieted. My writing days are over.

My only question is why I was so prompted in the beginning. Why didn't God choose a writer who could really write? Why pick a bumbling physician who had to steal minutes in the early morning darkness? I guess so I could learn a lesson: quit writing, you young fool. The truth has finally dawned on me: I am not a writer.

Wednesday, August 27, 1980

I am a fool. I cannot stop writing. It is a part of me.

I've progressed remarkably well as a Christian. I look holy for an hour a week in my white alb and then go out and live as the hypocrite that I really am.

I have two weeks left in the navy. I go to the naval hospital in the morning, wave, and leave to work in my town office. I show myself to the navy because I feel guilty, but I'm not missed. No one cares. I don't exist for the navy anymore.

When I get to the office my nerves go crazy as I see patient after patient. At 4:00 p.m. I stop to read EEGs for an hour and then I walk over to the hospital and see consults until 7:00 or 8:00. By the time I crawl in the door, Christine is already in bed. She looks at me like a stranger. Gretchen consoles me but I'm so emotionally wrung out I just want to respond to my bed as it calls to me from the bedroom. Before I can reach it the phone rings. Mrs. Treetop has a headache—the same one she has had for forty years.

Friday evening, August 29, 1980

Spiritual life is no fun. For that matter, life isn't much fun either.

Barbara Carey is dying of cancer. I went to pray fo her at the hospital yesterday. All her hair has fallen out and her weight has gone down. I sat with her, wearing my physician's coat, helpless, asking for God's help again.

I don't know why I continue to write. I know now that I'm not a good writer. And for whom am I writing? I had glowingly considered it was for God. He knows better than that. So I've decided spitefully to be passive-aggressive and not write for him anymore.

I think I'm grieving. Angry and grieving. My writing life is ending. My first book was a flop. This journal is my second. Another flop in the making. In my spare time I create flops.

Wednesday, September 10, 1980

I used to have a very organized life, but it has become chaotic. I don't pray anymore. (Perhaps I do once in awhile—a quickie.) My prayer time is now lost in morning rounds—seeing the sick and the dying. When I do pray I find myself wondering, with all those sick people around, if I wouldn't be more useful by their side than sitting in my chair thinking about scuba diving and calling it prayer?

It sounds very noble to visit the sick, except that the first thing I do with a new chart is check to see if the patient has insurance. If I see "none" or "Medicaid" I curse under my breath that this poor soul had to get sick my night on call. I see the patient anyway. He's a nine-year-old boy having repeated seizures. The hours pass as I try to decrease his intracranial pressure, stop the seizures. The parents look at me as if I'm trying to kill him. I save his life. There is a great sigh of relief. I receive neither a payment nor a thank-you. I go away with a headache, cursing medicine. I pass by a nun who smiles kindly. I smile back. She doesn't have to worry—God will provide. He just sends me the sick ones. Herein lies the joy of being a Christian: there isn't any.

The diaconate classes start in a week. I thought I was going to have to drop out for a while. Medicine is taking up all my time. When I eat I talk about patients. When I'm sleeping, I dream I'm making rounds. I get through at the hospital about the time the classes are over. I told Fausto God wants me to be a doctor. He said not to worry; the diocese wants to ordain me. What is wrong with those people? What do they see in me? Who am I?

Chapter 18

Come aside for a while

Wednesday, September 17, 1980

I feel as though a whirlwind has picked me up, spun me around, and dropped me back down in the rectory at Springhill College. It's like being back home, with a bit of peace and my typewriter.

I went to sign my papers last week to get out of the navy and as I was about to sign the final line they realized my orders had not arrived. The day before they had told me I would be out so I had mailed out announcements on the opening of my private practice. Good timing. They called Washington to explain the situation. "Oh, he doesn't even have a number yet."

So now I am in the navy with no job. I was told to report every day to say, "Good morning," and then I could leave. They are paying me to start my private practice. I can't complain. I guess at this point I could stand working with them for as long as they want to keep me—especially considering the way my practice is going.

Yesterday I made five dollars. Ten years of specialty training for five dollars. This is big-time neurology? I had a better day today, though. I made twenty-one dollars. In two weeks I'll be able to pay my secretary for one week of work.

So why not come to the rectory and live a few days with the Jesuits? I fit right in. A great deal of training and no money.

My mind is still spinning. I work until 8:00 every night except Friday when I don't schedule any time in the office. I registered for the diaconate courses and I've missed the first two weeks of classes. I've arranged with Fausto and the other teachers to take the courses by private study. With the transition into private practice I can't get there, or if I did I wouldn't be able to concentrate. I feel frustrated and guilty about the whole thing.

The main struggle I am having with my new medical practice is my battle with greed. I am terribly money-conscious, something I have hardly ever had to think about before. Fortunately I am so busy that I have stopped looking at the charts to see if the patients have insurance. But the next day....

These are the topics Father Rimes and I will probably be hashing over here at Springhill. I'm also going to do some of my diaconate class reading while I'm here.

Wednesday evening, September 17, 1980

Tonight was "Father Rector Night." Father Rimes was kind but advised that it might not be appropriate for me to attend, so that the Jesuits could get together as a group. I didn't mind.

I did get hungry, however, and crept into the private kitchen to make a sandwich. I left the light off so I wouldn't disturb the merry-making. Suddenly the light was flipped on and a tall, white-haired priest appeared in the doorway and asked me what I was doing. I explained that I was a candidate for the diaconate and I was making a retreat, and also a sandwich. He took my sandwich and threw it in the trash, saying, "You aren't going to eat this; come and join us." I squirmed uncomfortably and said I had not been invited. He replied that I was indeed invited and escorting me into the dining room, handed me a plate.

I excused myself and went to find Bob Rimes to explain that I didn't mean to interrupt. He smiled and said to make up a plate and eat in the other room. But the others wouldn't hear of it. They sat me down at the table and offered me champagne, a woven napkin, Dutch chocolate cake. I felt like kitchen help invited in to an elegant party. I was surprised that almost all the priests I had met last time still remembered my name is "Russ." At the conclusion of dinner I excused myself from the cigars and brandy (it really was a special occasion!) and returned to my room.

I don't know why I'm writing this. I guess I feel that Christ was present at that meal and he wanted me to join him. I felt very honored.

Thursday, September 18, 1980

Except for attending Mass with Father Rimes and a brief walk about the campus, I have spent the entire day reading. I finished the first volume of a history of Christian thought. At first I planned merely to skim the book but I got more and more interested in reading about the Apostolic Fathers, the heresies, and men such as Irenaeus, Tertullian, Clement, Origen, and others.

I met with Father Rimes for about an hour and told him of my greed for money. He said the devil will always begin his temptations with riches, not just financial riches, but good looks and so on—all those things the world finds charming and admirable. What we seek is not of this world, and the difficult part is the daily battle to remember that. Even if we seem to win, we still have to be careful or the devil may turn even our victory to his advantage, or trip us up with another temptation.

I find something exceedingly pleasant about Springhill College, a feeling I never experienced in college. It has an air of peace and friendliness, with smiles and hellos from strangers. There is more here than learning; there seems to be a stability and a way of life that can't be taught. I am very moved. Someday I might shock my ex-wife by offering to pay for my children to attend this college.

Sunday evening, November 16, 1980

Another diaconate weekend. The themes pervading our course-work now are discernment and pastoral counseling. Father Rimes spoke about discernment, using the writings of St. Ignatius. Fausto set me to work teaching part of one course entitled "Trouble spots in pastoral counseling." I hope I helped with my two hours of lecture.

I feel that I have been going through a period of desolation. My private practice has robbed me of my prayer life. No, that isn't true. I have *chosen* to let it rob me, to chase after money, to work until the late evening hours and miss my few minutes of prayer. I listen to tapes of spiritual songs on the way to work, and then I go into the hospital and rob people.

My life is filled with clutter. I have never seen so many patients. People are sick—broken physically, emotionally, and spiritually. God has given me certain gifts as a physician, and I am able to help some men and women, simply by caring and listening. I don't do a lot of curing, but I try to help people feel better.

I feel a tugging at my heart that can only be coming from God, an inner yearning for closeness. It brought me across the room tonight to this lonely typewriter.

Obviously my thoughts are scattered. My life is spread all over the place. Through it all I remain closest to Gretchen and Christine. They seem to wait for me, patient, understanding. I am very fortunate.

Tuesday, December 23, 1980
Altoona, Pennsylvania

Because of my new practice and the peculiar way my time is gobbled up, I have had to change my method of writing. I have started dictating notes to my secretary, Becky. It is a blessing to be able to share this part of my life with her.

How strange I must appear, sitting in front of this silly microphone. Even though I have a new way of doing this journal, I feel that the ink well has gone dry. I attempt to open my mind to God and all I hear is a car rumbling down the icy street and the clicking and spinning of the clothes dryer on the back porch.

At the moment we are visiting for a week in Pennsylvania with Gretchen's family. It is extremely dreary outside; the sky is gray and the temperature is twenty degrees with patches of ice on the road. Even here, though, the time is a blessed break from the rapid pace of my private practice. Finally, I'm away from hospital and patients long enough to sit for a few minutes and collect my thoughts. The odd part is that now that I'm here, microphone in hand, poised and ready, my mind is empty.

I continue to try to bring spirituality into my daily life and find myself failing nearly every day. Over the past month my only success has been setting Sunday mornings aside to pray with my neighbor, Barbara. Her cancer has become quiescent and her strength has returned. She is even walking again. It's amazing how she has changed during the past few months.

I remember how she looked when she was on the verge of death. I remember that night in the hospital when I listened to her shallow respirations and held her hand, feeling her grasp on life slipping away. As I prayed for her healing, both her eyes and mine were filled with tears. I prayed with the deepest sincerity I have ever felt. Something very special passed between us, feelings of impending loss, concern, love, and, I have to admit, a certain hopelessness. Personally I felt totally helpless. I knew our only hope was God. I prayed—I guess I begged—for her life and his help. I was unaware of anything at the time other than my own sincerity, which was refreshing. Often when I pray it's as if I'm only partly there, but that night I knew I was all there. I knew God had to have heard, but there were no flashes of light, no harps playing, and no angels singing; I merely prayed into the night and went home exhausted. I told Gretchen about my feelings and we went to sleep, holding each other, realizing the temporary grasp we have on our physical lives.

The next day Barbara was better. Over the next week her effusions started to melt away and her strength began to return. I will never argue with anyone about how this change came about; believers will know and unbelievers will think they know and suggest a logical theory. As far as I'm concerned I prayed along with many others. Prayers are important, but the praise belongs to God for listening.

Before this begins to sound too holy, I must share my true feelings. I am able to write the above with honesty and sincerity but I still feel like a spoiled, only child looking for some credit for myself. I would love to say, "I cured her," or that God cured her through my prayer. The closeness with God I crave would probably come much easier if I could simply stand back and let him do his thing. So there we have it. I want to swell with pride and banter about it. I guess I should thank God for even listening to me, knowing what sort of person I am. It's nice to know that God listens to a man like me.

Chapter 19

Reflections on the journey

Wednesday, Christmas eve, 1980

Snowflakes are beginning to fall. Memories return, as gentle as the evening snow, of Christmas two years ago when I brought communion to Gretchen's mother. In my infancy as a Christian, it was one of the most touching moments I can recall: the entire family kneeling on the kitchen floor, a solitary candle on the table, the love and the tears.

Since that walk in the snow I am two years closer to becoming a deacon, an ordained servant of God. Yet it seems that all I am interested in is serving myself.

Thursday, Christmas, 1980

Lord, today is your birthday. How does it make you feel? Are you happy?

There were hordes of people in your church this Christmas but I found myself asking, why so many today? Why so few during the year? True, a birthday is a celebration. We are a year older; we receive cards and gifts, usually a cake. But the next day our birthday is over and we go about our business as another year passes. I guess we look at your birthday in the same way. I wonder if our coming to church once a year in our Sunday best makes you happy.

How would a wife feel if her husband ignored her the entire year until her birthday or anniversary? Isn't it right to love her all year long and acknowledge that love with a special day? So often I have heard husbands—and I must confess that I myself, in my previous marriage, did the same thing—say, "I'd better give her something; it's her birthday." The gift is given out of a feeling of obligation rather than love. How great is the gift if we give only on one or two days a year when we feel a special obligation? Where is the love in such a relationship?

Sometimes I feel that Christmas for us has become just a chore, a bore, shopping, and baking. The Lord is not to be praised only once a year. He is timeless. "I will be with you always," he said. We live in time, so we can celebrate our birthday once a year, but he is, always, and we must praise him always. We err if we treat him as a once-a-year obligation. He will not be happy on such an occasion but will weep, for us.

Friday, December 26, 1980

Lord, at times I feel that I'm writing a letter to you. I mail it off to eternity and then I wait, not so patiently, for your reply. When your letter arrives it comes in words I cannot read, feelings I'm not sure of. But of one thing I am sure: every time I write I feel (and even somehow "see") others reading my words, somewhere in the future. It's as if my words are being reflected back to me through the eyes of others. I've never felt anything like it before.

I have asked myself many times why I am pouring myself out like this—why a simple physician who struggles with his faith and is so inept at writing it down, continues to try. You know my bitter disappointment at the failure of my first book, but somehow I am encouraged to write on, perhaps so my Jesuit friend, Father Rimes, can have something to read at the end of his busy day.

What I find myself struggling with, Lord, are your blessings, given to me for the benefit of others: the blessings of sharing in healing prayer; Christian friends; Gretchen and Christine; and even this writing. But I so easily fall into a state of desolation. Must I face a tragedy to force me to reach out and hold onto your hand? Would I, under such a circumstance, have the faith to reach out? Would I turn and curse you? My weakness is great. I am a very ordinary man.

Saturday, December 27, 1980

Lord, I am faced with many difficult decisions in my daily life. Even if I am to grow spiritually only to bring you into my practice of medicine, I will try. Sometimes I run into conflicts I seem unable to solve. I ask myself if I should be spending some time in prayer every day, alone in your presence, or if I should spend that time with a patient, being kind and caring. I fight with myself, Lord, about time. Teach me about time.

Perhaps I should pay attention to what I do with my time. My associate wants me to buy a CT head scanner with him, and then erect a building for the scanner. The goal, as far as I can see, is to make more money. Making money in itself is not bad, but I cannot see that I need more money. I would rather spend my time with you. I will need your help, though, to choose the right road.

Later in the day

For some reason I was looking up something in the Old Testament and came across a reading from Sirach on caution regarding associates. I was touched by this reading. Cautiously is the way I feel I must approach the CT head scanner situation. After all, how can the earthen pot go with the metal cauldron? When they knock together, the pot will be smashed.

Sunday, December 28, 1980

Our week with Gretchen's family is almost over. It has been a pleasant time of spiritual reflection, relaxation, and visiting.

I am already beginning to feel the unease of returning to work. The thought of making morning rounds depresses me. Then follows the brisk walk to the office, a half hour behind schedule, to find that three patients are already waiting. Finally, I see my last patient at 4:30 p.m. and face a stack of EEGs and MMPIs to be read. Then it's 5:30 and I have two consults to see at the hospital. Finally, the day ends at about 7:00 or 7:30 when I call Gretchen who is unbelievably cheerful. (I don't know whether I would be if our roles were reversed.) Christine has already gone to bed and I have missed her again. I drive home playing a spiritual tape but I barely hear the words. I am in a stupor. My mind is filled with the day's weary residue.

This is my life, Lord, the life I question and wonder about. I can't say I'm delighted and enthusiastic. I want to say I am depressed about it but I don't think I really am. The time seems to pass quickly during the day. I approach each patient as an individual. I know I am a good doctor, not an intellectual giant, but filled with a certain measure of care and empathy. It is most often on my way home that I ache inside from missing Gretchen and Christine. It is then that I feel that they are what life is all about, not the sickness and twisted emotions I see all day. I remind myself that in life thorns go with the roses.

So now I thank you for these past few days of peace with my family and friends. Give me the strength to go back and be what you want me to be.

Friday, January 2, 1981

Today is Christine's birthday. She is one year old already, an absolutely lovely baby.

This morning I had the strangest inclination to rewrite my first book. I am puzzled by this idea and have conflicting feelings about it. One problem is the struggle with time. I think the situation will probably take care of itself when I get back into the daily rat race of my practice.

Tuesday, January 6, 1981

I had better not have Becky type this page—she will certainly think I have lost my mind.

After rounds this morning I went to the hospital chapel to pray. It has been ages since I've done this. I went in, feeling that I am at a crossroad in my life because I have an urge to rewrite my first book. My goal in prayer was to open myself to God's will for me, rather than my own. I struggled to do this—to free my mind of my wants and needs so that I could listen. Eventually, a sister came in and dropped her sweater in my pew. Jokingly, she said, "I hope you won't take my sweater." It suddenly came to me that this morning I had rather nonchalantly walked off with a large roll of stamps from my associate's secretary. I hadn't felt right about taking the entire roll so I had replaced all but ten. In the chapel I suddenly envisioned myself walking in the aisle with Jesus. I felt that to get direction from him I had to walk with him and live like him. In other words, I would get my answer when I returned the rest of the stamps.

I came back to the office and put back the ten stamps, feeling a bit foolish. Even while I was dropping them back on the desk I was aware of wanting to take a short cut, to keep just one stamp. How absurd. Perhaps that is the way I am living—I am not really giving myself to God so he can work with me and guide me. I am stealing bits of myself away. Even holding back "one stamp's worth" is holding myself back.

The first step then must be to open myself to him. I have often thought of how my life (and probably that of others) reflects the Old Testament. Yahweh "saves" us as in the Exodus experience and we praise him and love him. But then the memory of the experience grows dim and we begin to turn away—not to Baal, but to our own material gods. We pray less because of television, yard work, and making more money. We rationalize and put things off until our world caves in. Then we reach out to God. How often I do this. I have done it today, again.

Tuesday, January 20, 1981

Today I was very touched by the fact that I belong to a nation that considers itself one under God. I have been sick all day so as I tossed and turned in bed I watched the inauguration of President Ronald Reagan. I guess in a way I have never really thought much about the country I live in: that I have the freedom to lie here and let my thoughts be free; that the government changes leadership so peacefully.

Saturday, January 31, 1981

Finally I have a day off. It has been a pleasure to sit by the fire today and listen to the rain outside, and have Christine paddling around, bringing her blanket to me and lying on my chest. It is good to stop along the journey and reflect.

The days have been passing in a sort of frantic but humdrum way, while I deal with seizures, back pain, headaches, and the complaints of people who are just plain miserable.

My morning prayer time has decreased to the few minutes that I visit the bathroom before leaving to make rounds. It really isn't a prayer at all but it's the only time I seem to have where my beeper isn't going off or the telephone isn't ringing. In those few moments I have been reading about Jeremiah. I'm certainly glad he had struggles with God. I can identify with them. Sometimes I feel that I'm being pulled inexorably toward God and a destiny that I don't understand and don't even want, but I have the ever-present hook in my mouth and the line is not about to break.

I sometimes wonder why I felt strongly that I should not read the lives of saints. I have often wanted to, but had the impression, "not yet; do not read about them now." Naturally, I've done just the opposite. A few months ago when I was in the library at Springhill I picked up a volume on Saint Teresa's writings. The book was so yellowed and tattered it could have been owned by Saint Teresa herself. I might as well have chosen a volume in Russian. I read but I couldn't comprehend; I had eyes but couldn't see. The words fogged. The experience was puzzling, to say the least, but now I think that reading about saints would be a fruitless undertaking. They are obviously beyond me at this point.

Jeremiah was a very human prophet and I am also very human—human to the point of doubt in my faith, rebellion, self-pity, and despair. Even as I want to summon others to grow and change, I stand in need of that same inward purification to grow and live in truth. At times I feel that my suffering is a share in Christ's suffering, a fellowship with divinity, flowing through my life. But I have a long journey ahead and so much to learn.

Sunday, February 1, 1981

I have just prayed with Barbara. It took a while after coming back to my house to settle myself. When I told Gretchen about our prayer, I started to cry.

I mentioned to Barb that prayers are often best when they are specific. When she asked me what we should pray about today, I directed her question back to her. She said she would like to pray for strength in dealing with her monthly chemotherapy. The adriamycin has caused her greater fear than the platinum, in that she can't stand the red color flowing into her. This past month, as they walked into the room with the IV setup and the medications, she began to shake and vomit before they even gave her the IV. So we decided we would pray about it today.

As we began to pray I reflected on being in the garden with Jesus and I felt for a moment that we were actually there, experiencing the terrible fear that Jesus felt before going to the cross. My stomach twisted with some of the agony, but what helped was the feeling that Jesus and I were together and that somehow there was a light at the end of the tunnel, that after three days he would rise again. Instead of our waiting for him in the garden, he would be with us at our own times in the garden, and the red adriamycin could be the flow of his life-giving blood into Barb, in her time of need. When we finished praying I was exhausted, tremulous, and my eyes were filled with tears. I felt that Barb would carry this experience with her to her next treatment, and that Jesus would help her somehow. The fear and the anxiety may be lessened if she can realize she is not alone in her ordeal.

After I related this to Gretchen we sat in front of the fire and held each other for a few minutes. She said she hoped that when our time to suffer comes, there will be somebody for us as there has been for Barb.

Sunday, February 8, 1981

My prayers continue weekly for Terry and for Barb. I find that praying for healing against cancer takes a great deal of effort. After prayer I always feel fatigue, but also a lightening of the spirit. Terry has not had a seizure in several months. He continues to feel well and he looks great. At times I believe that his healing is as much for me as it is for him. I am really pleased about his progress. It is obvious to me that physicians must, from time to time, ask for help.

Thursday, February 19, 1981

On Sunday I prayed again with Barb. I have felt all along that she is attracted to a spiritual life but is like an outsider looking in. She cannot seem to allow herself to ask for help so we prayed again that she somehow be able to share her suffering with Christ, to identify with the suffering that he went through. I found myself explaining that if she would spend ten minutes a day in prayer or meditation, it would also provide time for God to work with her. We don't have to do all the talking. (As I was saying this I realized that I have not been praying very much lately myself.) When I told her I had slipped out of my daily prayer pattern, she offered to pray for me. She seemed very enthusiastic about it and I thought that if she could do it, then I could too, so we promised that we would pray for each other this week for at least ten minutes a day. Her next chemotherapy treatment is this Friday and we prayed that she would be able to face it with more strength and less anxiety.

Meanwhile Terry has been doing extremely well. He feels good and his wife is pregnant. They are delighted. Terry and I have continued to meet weekly and spend a few minutes in prayer. I find it difficult to believe how well he has done.

Friday, February 20, 1981

This seems an unlikely place to write. We are twenty-five stories high in a marvelous hotel in Hawaii, overlooking a wide expanse of blue-green Pacific Ocean. Gretchen and I are here for a meeting on MMPIs; she hopes to learn how to score them and I hope to learn more about interpretation. We are also here to celebrate our wedding anniversary. I think God has come with us.

As our jumbo jet was heading down the runway to take off from San Diego, I was telling Gretchen how excited I was to get away and have time to rest, relax, and enjoy the sunshine, when she looked across the aisle and said that someone appeared to have passed out.

It was obvious the man had lost consciousness. He was pale and his wife was applying an air sickness bag to his face. We had not left the ground yet but I knew that if he didn't get his head down he would start having seizures. I left my seat, moved the man's wife out of hers, and put her next to Gretchen. I sat down next to the man and quickly pulled him as far onto my lap as possible. I was aware of many eyes watching what was going on. The plane was leaving the ground and the pressure of the takeoff was forcing me into my seat. Suddenly the man started to jerk and twitch. Then his eyes popped open and he looked extremely confused. I leaned him back and he began sweating profusely. He fell against me briefly and then sat bolt upright again. I tried to get him to relax. A moment later a stewardess arrived with oxygen and a cold towel. The pilot came back and asked me whether we should turn around, but by that time it seemed he was all right and we could continue. During the time this was going on I had been completely cool and calculating, thinking that God must have arranged our seats in this way, but when it was over I felt as if I had turned to jelly. My appetite was gone and I was extremely fatigued. God uses my talents, but sometimes I swear he wears me out.

As we were landing in Hawaii the stewardess gave Gretchen and me a complimentary bottle of champagne for what we had done and many of the people on the flight congratulated me for "my work."

I silently congratulated God on his work. He should have the praise and the champagne, for continuing to work through history and nature. I guess in some ways God never takes a vacation. What love he has for his flock.

Saturday, February 28, 1981

This afternoon we leave Hawaii. It was really nice to take time out for ourselves.

Sometimes I think I take too much for granted. My life gets wrapped up in paying the bills, buying groceries, seeing another patient, making another dollar. While I'm running in circles, sometimes I miss my child who toddles by and looks out the window at the palm trees and the water with wonder in her eyes. I miss the simple beauty while she smiles at a bird, or picks a flower and sniffs the fresh scent.

On a trip like this I often think about Jesus, when he took a week or a day and disappeared into the desert. No one knows what he did during those times. I suppose most people feel that he prayed for twenty-four hours, which he may have. I like to think that he sometimes took a few hours for himself, to sit under a tree and rest. It's what we all need from time to time to make life fresh again. It gives me a chance to look at the person I married and just be with her and appreciate her.

So now it's time to say goodbye to the coconut trees and the University of Hawaii where we spent much of the week. I love being around universities where everyone is learning. I guess it's because I've spent three-quarters of my life in that environment. Still the learning goes on. I pray that I never stop learning about the spiritual life, as hard as it is for a man like me.

Thursday, March 5, 1981

Lately I am becoming concerned for our diaconate program. As ordination draws closer there is a natural anticipation and excitement filling the air. What I have heard lately, though, dampens the excitement. Some of our newly ordained deacons have been described as "stuck up," and "those pompous know-it-alls who act as though they are better than God." One deacon who preached about marital fidelity is having an affair. Most of the deacons seem to think they are better than the priests. One deacon threatened a priest that if he didn't allow him to give a homily he was going to leave the Church. Hearing such things makes me wonder what we are doing.

Just today I met a doctor's assistant at the hospital who commented that several people in her parish are going to another because they can't stand the way the deacons act. "They are self-centered; they act so holy they are driving people crazy."

I can relate to some of the problems. They remind me of when I was an intern, freshly graduated from medical school. The interns at the hospital (including myself) all acted as if we were the brightest young doctors on earth. We knew everything; we could handle everything. We thought our professors and staff doctors were senile. It didn't take us long to realize that we were again at the bottom of the barrel and that we had a long way to go to be able to do heart surgery and diagnose strokes of the brainstem. After our initial bout of grandiosity most of us became humble again, although there were always exceptions. But we never threatened that if we couldn't operate on a heart we would leave medicine. It seems so absurd to threaten to leave the Church if we aren't allowed to preach. I fear that we have not become very good at showing what a deacon is.

Sunday, March 8, 1981

Last week was incredibly complex. I don't think I have ever been so overwhelmed with the business aspect of my work. The patients came and went almost without notice as I made decisions about incorporating my business, hiring another secretary, buying a car, and on and on.

By Friday afternoon when my colleague and I went to lunch, I had reached the point where I had to tell him that I didn't feel comfortable committing myself to buy part of a head scanner. It was as if the entire week had been consumed by plans for time and money, and though I had attempted to pray about the project, I didn't get anywhere. Gretchen and I had talked about it and we knew the investment just didn't fit me. As I spoke to my colleague I began to feel like myself again. My interest in writing started to return and my interest in church involvement came back.

What amazes me is that I believe there is a spiritual side to a week like this. It's very subtle. In fact, it is so subtle and so global at the same time that we often don't see it. We are so consumed by all the opportunities that crop up (some of which promise fame or money) that we find them almost irresistible. But while we are following these passions we are really taking a step away from God. I certainly have been. I've been going through one of the lowest lows I've had in ages.

I realize now that I have been approaching ordination and at the same time moving away from God by chasing pots of gold. One of the goals I want to set for myself is to begin morning prayer again with the help of the Office, a book of readings and prayer to sanctify the day, which priests are required to pray daily. One can really turn to it any time of day, but I would like to pray it in the morning. If I don't do it then, I won't do it at all.

Wednesday, March 25, 1981

So much has been happening the past three weeks I haven't had time to think, much less pray.

There has been a great deal of turmoil at work, which has driven me to the point of renting an office next door and trying a practice on my own. Two offices under one roof hasn't worked.

Later this afternoon I have an interview with the bishop about ordination. I don't know what to think at this point. I feel in some ways that if I'm not accepted I will be disappointed but at the same time it won't be the end of the world, either. If I am accepted, a whole new world opens up for me. In a few hours I'll know.

Thursday, March 26, 1981

The bishop has accepted me for ordination. I was really excited to hear the news. He asked me to pray for what I could do in the Church but I think we both know that I will be working in the diaconate training program. It sounds as though I might also be teaching a pastoral counseling course next year. I can't believe all this is happening. Three years ago I was basically nothing; now I'm going to be an ordained minister. God works in strange ways.

Chapter 20
Tomorrow is forever

...Carry out everything I have commanded you. And know that I am with you always, until the end of the world! *Matthew 28:20*

Friday evening, April 3, 1981

I can't believe I'm back here in Panama City where this journey began for me. It seems such a short time ago that I drove down in the back of a van with a group of strangers to find out about the diaconate program. It was here that I first met Father Fausto and felt the love in the program along with the urging of my own spirit to join it.

Now I am back at the same motel three years later for the last meeting of the year—the meeting during which we come aside for a while and prepare for our ordination. Gretchen and I are both amazed at what has happened in the past three years. She has been at my side the entire time and I realize that none of this would have happened without her. Without knowing it, she led me to the Church, to the diaconate program, and to ordination.

As usual, tonight we were all tired when we celebrated mass, but despite our fatigue, our jobs and families, our duties and responsibilities, we were here. We all managed to take the time to be with God and to prepare ourselves.

I feel right now that I have been stopped in my tracks. The events of the past two months, building my private practice and dealing with the office hassles, have consumed my mind and spirit. My meeting with the bishop was a side step and then I was right back into the office problems. My life has been nothing but ordering equipment, arguing, and trying somehow to keep seeing patients, putting one foot in front of the other.

Saturday morning, April 4, 1981

I am writing these notes as events are happening.

We have started the day with Father Rimes who is leading the retreat for those who are to be ordained, sixteen ordinary men called by God.

Father Rimes began, interestingly enough, with my thoughts of last night. At times like this, he said, it is important to follow Jesus, to come aside for a while and be with him. Just as Jesus went into the desert to pray and to be with his father, we must also spend some time alone. Father Rimes began with a quotation from Matthew 6:21: "Remember, where your treasure is, there your heart is also." Our theme is to find ourselves, to find where our treasure and our hearts really are. (I remember seeing that passage written in Pat's office on my first visit to him—and now here it is again.)

Father Rimes has always been an inspiration to us. When he says Jesus loves us with an everlasting love, for whatever we are, somehow we feel the truth of those words. He said we must leave our cares where they are; they will still be there. We must be like the lilies of the field which do not toil or spin. Too much of our time is fretted away as it is.

Also, Father Rimes told us it is important to remember that becoming a deacon is not the end; it is the means to an end. God is calling us for something; it is important to concentrate on our own lives, where we began, where we are going. We must open ourselves to communicate with our God. From the moment of conception God knew us and loved us with an everlasting love. From his point of view we are lovable. He wants us to be ourselves and not someone else. The purpose of our existence is to live with and in God's plan for us. If we wander away, we are not punished; we simply go astray and God brings us back, because God is love.

God continues to love us, to further enhance us. It is easy to think of ourselves as insignificant specks on this earth but our call to ministry is a real call. We will receive a true sacrament, an internal mark, like the one we received at baptism.

I am sitting in the sunshine now with only my writing tablet. I have a half-hour for private meditation. The sunshine has always been a peaceful place of refuge for me. At the moment I am gazing at tufts of grass and little shrubs growing out of the sand. I can almost see it as a desert. Jesus is here with his disciples who are also staring at the sand, wondering who is this person whom they are following.

What does Jesus have in store for me? I am irresistibly attracted to him, but where is he leading me? I meet some men who say with certainty that they know their ministry. But I don't know mine, even though I have a title. As far as I can see I will become psychiatric consultant to the diaconate formation program and to the clergy. But I feel so unbelievably low, almost in terror of what I am facing.

Saturday, April 4, 1981, noon

Some of what Father Rimes is saying to us I am writing down, because it will do me good to remember it.

When responding to God we must know that our way is not necessarily his. Through his Holy Spirit he teaches us. God is the potter and we are the clay. The person called has the primary responsibility of saying yes to the call. Our response must be offered in love.

At the same time, some human mediators are necessary for spiritual direction. To be a formation director, as Father Rimes admits, is thrilling and humbling. "We watch the mystery of God in action, but somehow we do more than watch; it is as if we are copresent with God, in time with him, and also with the individual trying to grow." The spiritual director's task is to facilitate without imposing personal views.

The Father continues the work of his son through us. Most of us err by either demeaning ourselves or being vain and proud. Being loved by a mate is a humbling experience, not something to be vain or arrogant about, and so it should be with our relationship with God.

The glory of God is man and woman, fully alive. God's gift of life to us is not just for our own sake. It is also meant for others who may be dependent for their salvation on what God manifests in us.

Saturday afternoon, April 4, 1981

I am alone again, back in the sunshine with my own thoughts threading their way back to psychiatry. I was frustrated with the idea of being a "catalyst" in psychiatry. Yet that is apparently what God has called me to be—a thankless but beautiful catalyst to bring people to one another and to God. He gave me a gift to facilitate communication; obviously I did not train in psychiatry in vain.

I still feel frightened of my role but I can't think of any other one to play. I am afraid of being a deacon. I am afraid of being a deacon physician at a Catholic hospital. How will people see me? How do I see myself? Can I be myself? Am I going to walk around a foot off the ground feeling holy, or am I going to crawl through the cracks hoping nobody sees me?

Perhaps there will be something about me that resembles Jesus. I may never realize the role I am playing in the lives of my patients, my secretaries, nurses, and colleagues. At times I may be criticized and ridiculed. Many will not know me and others will think they know me and put me on a pedestal. Through it all I write on, faithfully, foolishly.

Father Rimes said Ignatius prayed for years, "Place me with your son." What most impressed me was that when Ignatius finally received his answer after years of prayer, he knew he was answered but he did not know what it meant! He saw Jesus bearing a cross on his back on the road to Rome and Ignatius thought it might mean his own crucifixtion. He didn't know what would happen but he felt he had an answer. I often feel this way, that I have an answer but I don't know what it means.

This calling to orders, this invitation to Christ, the knowledge that he will give me what I need, I find overwhelming. His anointing will touch my inner being. I don't know how but I know it will affect my activity. I'm not going to get a mark on my soul that will wash off. I won't be able to put it on and take it off as I choose. It will remain with me the rest of my life. The ordination is a visible outward sign of God; I will become an outward sign of Christ the priest.

Despite my fears, on the day of ordination I know I will answer yes to the call. My answer was yes the day I began this writing.

Tuesday, April 7, 1981

I just received the report of Terry's CT head scan. There has been no change in the appearance since September 1979. He still has a persistent, low density, right frontal lesion but he hasn't been having seizures. He continues to do very well, and now works part-time at the hospital as a volunteer.

I haven't seen Barbara in almost two weeks but she has just about finished her chemotherapy treatment course and is doing amazingly well.

I thank God for what he has accomplished in their lives.

Wednesday morning, April 8, 1981

I'm really dragging this morning. Every night now when I get home I have been trying to study for our finals in the synoptic Gospels and the history of Christian thought. Last night I went through Luther and Calvin and by the time I finished I couldn't distinguish one from the other. I have an oral final exam on Friday and I hope I will be better prepared.

I finally had some time this morning after rounds to get to the hospital chapel. I have really missed my daily visits there. Now I feel almost a stranger when I walk in and sit down.

I prayed this morning for my associate. The past few days we have exchanged few words. We do our work at either end of the hall and pass quietly in between. I've tried to work with him in every way I can but there seems to be resistance at every turn. I prayed for peace in that we might continue somehow to work together and not grow further apart.

Suddenly I thought of Jesus' saying, "It is easier for a camel to pass through the eye of a needle than for a rich man to enter the kingdom of God." But for God all things are possible and I continue to pray.

Friday evening, April 10, 1981

I had my oral exam today in the history of Christian thought. I'm glad it's over.

Palm Sunday, April 12, 1981

I'm on my way to Boston for a course on learning disabilities in children. Since I am consulting now for the Escambia County School System I thought I should sharpen my skills a bit, though I'm more excited about seeing Pat again. Wednesday evening I will fly to Philadelphia and visit with him until Saturday. The navy has assigned him there for two years of post-graduate training in theology. I really need this time away to continue my prayers and thoughts about ordination. It seems awesome to me.

Yesterday a story about me appeared in the newspaper. It was unbelievable—a five by seven photograph with an account of my conversion. I have never experienced such a day on rounds. People stared at me; a surgeon who has never spoken to me came up and shook my hand; patients who were not my own spoke to me about how the article impressed them. Other people called the office. One woman thanked me because it somehow "inspired" her twenty-two-year-old son who had drifted away from the Church. Still others, mostly my colleagues, went out of their way to avoid me. God is working. I am fortunate to be an instrument to touch others.

Monday morning, April 13, 1981

I think it is best after the publicity to leave town immediately for a week. Gretchen says I have received several phone calls from people who can identify with me since reading my "testimony" in the paper.

A woman who had drifted away from the Church since the death of her husband wants to talk to me. Why me, for heaven's sake? I have done nothing except become a convert—a shaky one at that.

My mother also called. She said I "made my parents sound bad," and that I was "overdramatic." She thought I had invented most of the article from an "overly-active imagination."

Publicity is hard for me. I love it and I can't stand it. It goes to my head and intoxicates me and at the same time I get the urge to leave town, to hide. When it brings people to me I feel insecure, as if I have to be someone I'm not. But God wants us to be only who we are—to be fully ourselves; to acknowledge our weakness and our errors; to ask his help. So if this woman comes to me I will listen and do what I can, and ask his help along the way.

Tuesday evening, April 14, 1981

Boston is windy and rainy. I'll be glad to move on to Philadelphia.

After two days of hearing about learning disorders in children I am convinced we don't know anything at all about the subject. One of our speakers summed up his hour and a half lecture on cerebral dominance by saying, "The possibilities are intriguing, but clinically what we've learned so far doesn't help at all."

Gretchen spoke with Becky today. The office has been flooded with phone calls in response to the article in the paper. People want to talk to a "Christian psychiatrist." I'm only doing a limited amount of psychiatry, though, so Becky had to turn most of them away.

I miss Gretchen. I like getting away from the office but I surely miss her.

I cannot sleep. I just watched a TV production of *Peter and Paul* which was well done. I was pleased to see that these men were portrayed as having doubts and uncertainties almost as great as their faith.

Lord, uncertainty and doubt plague me. As my ordination grows near I feel an overwhelming sense of inadequacy and unworthiness. I pray that I will be of service to you—that I will follow you and your will for me. Yet I am weak. It is now that I need you. Help me.

Good Friday, April 17, 1981, 9:00 a.m.

Last night Pat and I had a marvelous time. We celebrated mass and I read the renewal of commitment to priestly service for Pat and another priest. It began with the words, "My brothers." Suddenly I felt I was indeed going to become a brother with them.

After mass we went to a restaurant for dinner. Right there in the middle of the hubbub, Pat said, "Let's pray." For a few seconds we prayed for my coming ministry and their anniversary.

In a lighter moment, Pat decided to offer a special blessing for all those whom he sees just once a year at Easter or Christmas. He will never change.

6:00 p.m.

Pat asked me to read the part of Jesus in the Passion narrative. I was touched. There I was, the least of all the ministers, entering the lives of the congregation. Isn't that how Jesus so often presents himself—just where we least expect to find him? I found the liturgy very moving.

We have had a good visit. I love Pat. He gave me an entire set of the Liturgy of the Hours which I am going to try using for daily prayer and meditation. The problem is I can't figure out the sequence of the prayers.

Saturday, May 2, 1981

I have been back for a week already. A busy, racing week.

Preparations are under way for the weekend of ordination, two weeks from today. There will be a grand reception afterwards and our parish is making plans for more celebration. I will attend Saturday evening mass for the first time as a deacon on May 16. I will read the Gospel and perhaps even say a few words. Sunday at our own parish there will be a mass of thanksgiving.

I am excited as the time grows near. I have started praying the Liturgy of the Hours (Office) in preparation. I have generally been able to do the readings and morning and evening prayer. The rest of my day is spent on neurology.

Since moving into my own office I have noticed a subtle change in myself. I am beginning to practice medicine in the way I have always done it best, with love and patience. Oh, I do hurry; I do get behind. I say "damn" and occasionally use some other more colorful terms. But I also listen to what I am being told. I talk with families. I spend a little extra time on rounds for that extra measure of care. And it's in that extra measure of care and concern that love and empathy begin to emerge.

Thursday night I was called to see an exdeacon, of all people. His life has collapsed over the past few years with a back injury, a divorce, and now a fall resulting in a pulmonary embolus. It was after 7:00 p.m. when I walked into his room, the last place I wanted to be. I was hungry, tired, and emotionally drained. I wanted to be with Gretchen and Christine. This was going to be the third night in a row that I hadn't seen my daughter.

The former deacon had more problems than I did. He was having attacks of being unable to swallow that I recognized as manifestations of anxiety. He was afraid of dying. For the past few years he had been piecing his life back together and it had come tumbling down again. His goal of attending law school in the fall seemed eons away after it had been almost within his grasp.

Listening to him I felt that if his life were mine I would find it hard to swallow. "Hard to swallow!" I spoke my thoughts out loud. He realized this described how he felt. We went on to talk about how easy it would be at this point to regress—take a step backward. To be sick would be less traumatic than taking that step into the unknown—back into life. We talked seriously, our eyes locked. My weariness evaporated. God gave me that extra ounce of strength. When we stopped talking a few minutes later he thanked me and said, "You are all that I thought you would be from the newspaper article."

I wish I could reconcile the person who walked into the room, irritated, tired, and not wanting to be there, to the one described in the article, who left the room in peace. I am both of these people. But it is God who brings the peace.

Sunday, May 3, 1981

Today we have a practice session after mass for a deacon's duties during mass. How many rehearsals must we have? The whole process of becoming a deacon is beginning to remind me of training to be a surgeon. As a medical student you begin by watching from a distance. When it is seen you will not pass out at the sight of blood (it happens), you are allowed to assist in removing the spleen of a dog. If the dog survives you get to reach over a shoulder in the operating room and hold a retractor. As an intern you get a larger retractor or you hold one in both hands. As a surgery resident you begin to sew—everything: your sheets, your pants, the turkey, and occasionally skin. As the years pass you do a bit more until suddenly you are alone, making the incision into someone who is now trusting you with his or her life.

Now here I am, finally about to read the Holy Gospel to the people, to put my life on display in front of the Church. Three years ago I was nothing. I didn't know when to sit or when to stand. I didn't know the words to prayers. I mumbled and hummed (mostly off key) through hymns of worship. (At times I still do.) My God, look at where you have brought me, and where you have brought my deacon colleagues!

Tuesday, May 12, 1981

After three years of work, suddenly ordination is coming faster than I can believe. I don't feel particularly well at the moment. I've had a virus all week and have lost my voice. Now today I've got an infection in my eye. I'll be a wreck for the ordination if this continues.

Pat Fryer is going to come down Friday night to be with us for the ordination and the rest of the weekend. I don't think everything will hit me until the weekend is over.

Wednesday, May 13, 1981

Today as Pope John Paul II greeted fifteen thousand tourists and faithful at his weekly audience in St. Peter's Square he was shot by a gunman. The pope was beaming and waving at the crowd in the sunlit square when suddenly shots were fired and he slumped in his white jeep. Blood began to stain his white garments and the horrified witnesses cried, "Oh no! Oh no!" Two women in the crowd were also wounded.

Rumors were rampant for the first two hours. He was critical; he had been shot twice, four times, in the neck, in the chest, in the arm. Finally it was learned that he had survived approximately six wounds. The prognosis is guarded because of post-operative risks of infection.

Police quickly arrested a man identified as a right-wing Turkish terrorist who had once vowed to kill the pope. He told the police that he "couldn't care less about life." World leaders were stunned, expressing horror and outrage. Worshippers all over the world prayed and lit candles in thousands of Roman Catholic churches.

I think that for many the attack on John Paul II was an ugly flashback to the still-fresh memories of President Reagan's attempted assassination six weeks ago. Unfortunately, this is our world. Now bullets have felled a man of peace, who prayed for an end to war and to terrorism, who sought to improve the condition of all people. My prayers are with him.

Thursday, May 14, 1981

The pope is recovering, thank God. I offered my morning prayer for him.

I feel a bit of pride to be able to stand up in the robes of a cleric this weekend and show myself to the world as another man of peace, to share in such a beautiful ministry, so hated by some of the world. Such a calling is indeed glorious.

Friday, May 15, 1981

Suddenly I am overwhelmed with anxiety. My skin is crawling, my stomach is jumping, my bowels are running. I am filled with awe. Where has the time gone?

I thought that when ordination finally came I would be on top of everything. I would be prayerful, filled with self-confidence and holiness.

Now I look at myself almost painfully, realizing that the last several months have probably been the worst I have had in the last three years. My prayer life has become almost nonexistent. I read the Office every morning and evening. Minutes later I cannot recall what I have read. I have not sat in silence to listen, to be with God, more than a few minutes a day. I do not feel self-confident. The private practice that I started has folded around me; the colleague with whom I began is barely an acquaintance. The thought of holiness brings a weary smile to my face. I realize now that I am not filled with anything but fluttering butterflies and nagging doubts.

I cannot believe that I am actually going to be a cleric, an ordained, permanent deacon for life. Along with my anxieties, though, I am excited, thrilled, and soaring. I don't think I have ever approached a day filled with so much meaning.

My friends and Gretchen have been wonderful. I have received lovely cards and prayers. Almost all our friends, Catholic and non-Catholic, are coming to the ordination. My parents don't think they will make it—it's too early in the morning and my mother doesn't have a hat.

Gretchen is excited. She has worked nearly all week (with some help from her friends) making my dalmatic. We are both delighted that Pat is coming tonight to share tomorrow with us. Gretchen and Pat are the two corners of my trinity. The thought of my love for them brings tears to my eyes. I'm afraid that tomorrow the tears are going to flow. My God, you have brought me life where there was no life.

I'm afraid I'm not going to be a very good minister. I have always struggled with giving myself to others. I don't expect ordination to change my fundamental personality but I know that I must be here for a reason. Perhaps, like the recent newspaper article, my ordination will somehow be God's instrument to stimulate others to grow in spiritual life. While I flounder with my own spirituality, perhaps others seeing me will be moved to do something with their own lives. I may always struggle to understand my life's purpose and to pray and serve the Lord, but through it all I hope God will be visible in my actions and my words. I want to be Christ-like.

At times I still find it difficult even to praise God, the very one who has given everything to me. I hope at such times I can remember the words of St. Augustine, "Let us love God with the love he has given us; if you desire to praise him, then live good lives and you will be his praise." I can identify with those words because I know I have love. If I can realize this love has come from God I will find it easy to return. If my life can express this love then I will not need words: I will *be* God's praise. This is my goal.

For some time now I have had an internal awareness that this page is the last one for this book, a symbol of the end of my lay life. Tomorrow a new life begins for me, a new chapter in a new book. I don't know what life will bring, but I know it will change. God doesn't allow us to go through all these events without a purpose. These words end a chapter in my life, a chapter of conversion and struggle, a chapter of growth and of love.

As I begin this new journey I pray that I can follow God's will, that I won't stray with the pride that always seems to dog my footsteps. I pray that I will not travel with such intense concentration on a goal that I cannot take time to enjoy the wonders along the way, the tiny everyday marvels that call us to stop a while and celebrate, and praise God for the journey as well as the destination. I thank you, Lord, for the journey.

Words, like an echo, are moving through my mind, words I will begin to live tomorrow: "Receive the Gospel of Christ, whose herald you are. Believe what you read, teach what you believe, and practice what you preach."

My God, tomorrow is forever.

Epilogue

Terry Wilson died December 9, 1982

Barbara Carey died July 22, 1983

The author was asked by their families to preside over both funerals as a deacon.

Affirmation Books is an important part of the ministry of the House of Affirmation, International Therapeutic Center for Clergy and Religious, founded by Sr. Anna Polcino, S.C.M.M., M.D. Income from the sale of Affirmation books and tapes is used to provide care for priest and religious suffering from emotional unrest.

The House of Affirmation provides a threefold program of service, education, and research. Among its services are five residential therapeutic communities and two consulting centers in the United States and one residential center in England. All centers provide nonresidential counseling. The House sponsors a leadership conference each year during the first week of February and a month-long Institute of Applied Psychothcology during July. More than forty clinical staff members conduct workshops and symposiums throughout the year.

For further information, write or call the administrative offices in Boston, Massachusetts:
>
> The House of Affirmation
> 22 The Fenway
> Boston, Massachusetts 02215
> 617Œ266-8792